CIVIL WAR
GHOSTS OF
CENTRAL GEORGIA
AND SAVANNAH

CIVIL WAR
GHOSTS OF
CENTRAL GEORGIA
AND SAVANNAH

JIM MILES

Haunted America

Published by Haunted America

A Division of The History Press

Charleston, SC 29403

www.historypress.net

First published 2013

Manufactured in the United States

ISBN 978.1.62619.191.4

Library of Congress CIP data applied for.

For the aunts: Flora Craven, Dink Ridgeway, Joann Hawkins and Lindy Bayles.

CONTENTS

INTRODUCTION

Civil War historians concentrate on northern Georgia and Atlanta, where the great battle of Chickamauga and the multiple conflicts resulting in the conquest of Atlanta—one of the Confederacy's most important manufacturing centers—occurred. But Georgia is a huge state, the largest east of the Mississippi River, and much important Civil War activity occurred in the two-thirds of Georgia found in the central, coastal, and southern parts of the state.

Sherman's March to the Sea is a classic campaign studied in military schools worldwide and decisive in the American Civil War. William Sherman occupied Atlanta for several months before chasing John Hood into northern Alabama. He then returned to Atlanta to plan his next campaign. Sherman picked sixty thousand battle-hardened veterans to march across Georgia to the Atlantic Ocean at Savannah. Sherman's March is famous in Civil War history. The Federals ripped the heart out of the Confederacy, devastating a region sixty miles wide and three hundred miles long, proving the war was nearly over.

Savannah is one of America's most interesting cities, and much of its history is devoted to the struggle to safeguard the port during the war. Savannah has long been a major American port, dating back to colonial days. As a Confederate port, Savannah was effectively sealed off from blockade runners, but because the city was approached by rivers and guarded by swamps, it held out until Sherman's army arrived in December 1864. Savannah has been called "America's Most Haunted City," and many of the city's ghosts belong to the Civil War era. Some haunt Savannah's well-preserved forts, while others are found in the many old houses, hotels and cemeteries.

Central Georgia, which contains well over half of Georgia, includes two of the Confederacy's major industrial cities—Columbus and Macon—which produced considerable weapons and other military goods. The area also contains the farmlands that provided troops in both the western and eastern theaters with nourishment. Because military action reached the region only late in the war, little was destroyed and much remains preserved. Columbus and West Point fell after Lee's surrender, and the same Union cavalry raid that took those cities ended in Macon without a shot fired. In the last act of the war, Confederate president Jefferson Davis entered the region seeking escape from Federal pursuers, but he was captured at Irwinville.

As the war progressed, the Confederacy was faced with a serious problem. Many Union soldiers had been captured, but more of the fledgling nation was vulnerable to attack and raids. Also, the Federals, noting that they could easily replace lost prisoners while the Confederacy could not, began a policy of not exchanging prisoners. Andersonville prison, a large prisoner of war camp located deep in Georgia, fatally lacked clean water, adequate food and decent shelter. By the time this tragic situation played out, thirteen thousand Union prisoners had died.

Throughout this region, thousands of wounded and ill soldiers received care in hospital centers.

Death and misery plagued this part of Georgia, and the ghosts of soldiers killed by battle, inadequate medical care and deprivation in prisons haunt rural areas, small towns and cities. Civil War ghosts abound, concentrated on battlefields, prison sites and hospital centers.

PART I

PHANTOMS ALONG SHERMAN'S MARCH

Sherman's March was a grand, largely carefree campaign to the overpowering Federals, and the worst nightmare for the defenseless civilian population. This campaign still haunts the South, and it left a number of ghosts in its wake.

HENRY COUNTY

The End of the Atlanta Campaign, the Beginning of Sherman's March

The eastern edge of Henry County is bordered by the South River. People could cross the stream on Butler's Bridge until it was dismantled. C.W. Hollingsworth owned a dairy farm that bordered the bridge.

"It was always a spooky place," his grandson Wes stated. "A lot of people didn't like it, even in the daytime."

C.W. told Wes that Union troops used Butler's Bridge Road at the start of Sherman's March. The Union general sent an advance guard of ten scouts to examine the route. The scouts were captured, probably while looting, and hanged from trees by their Confederate captors. A local legend said if someone went there on a dark night and sang "Dixie," the bodies of the executed men would appear, dangling from old oak trees.

On a daring teenaged expedition, Wes and buddies went to the bridge on a dark night, a cassette tape blaring "Dixie" on the stereo. As the song played, the boys saw the bodies hanging from the trees all around them.

Wes said some locals refused to cross the bridge after midnight, and stories were told of cars stalling on the span and terrified stranded motorists seeing ghostly apparitions and hearing the sounds of combat and fighting.

"There's always been something down there you can't understand," Wes said. "It's a weird place."

Sherman's Right Wing, under Major General Oliver O. Howard, left Atlanta for Savannah via the McDonough Road and passed through McDonough on November 15–16, 1864. Skirmishes between Federal cavalry under Judson Kilpatrick and Confederate cavalry commanded by Alfred Iverson occurred on the edges of the march. Federals burned two churches, slaughtered animals in a third and destroyed mills as they progressed.

NEWTON COUNTY

Gaither: The Plantation Visited by Sherman's Bummers

During mid-November 1864, one of the four columns of Sherman's army, numbering fifteen thousand men, swept through Newton County like a plague of locusts, stealing food, fodder and personal treasures, and torching much of what they could not carry away. A thin scattering of Confederates withdrew before this inexorable wave, and it is believed that several hid at the Gaither Plantation until the Federals passed.

One day several years ago, during a wedding celebration, a ghostly apparition dressed in a gray uniform, presumably a Confederate, was seen in the basement. A search revealed no one present. On another occasion, a reenactor in full uniform observed not a dead Confederate, but a woman, rocking and nursing an infant in an upstairs bedroom.

Amber Pittman, reporter for the *Covington News*, was told that Confederates had been hidden in the attic, where footsteps thought to belong to the soldiers are heard. Also, "shadow people" that are believed to be the spirits of Southern soldiers have been observed walking the grounds.

The Gaither Plantation has invited a number of ghost investigation organizations to hunt the farm, and abundant evidence of supernatural encounters has been collected. One group was the Georgia Paranormal

Research Team from Dublin. During their EVP session, a spirit identified himself as a Confederate soldier.

Newton County was fortunate to be able to purchase the Gaither house, several outbuildings and two hundred acres of the former plantation. A 1916 church from nearby Social Circle has been relocated to the property. The Friends of Gaither Plantation was formed to administer the estate, which is available for weddings, reunions, festivals, tours and other events.

The Haunted Halls of Oxford College

Just north of Covington, in the community of Oxford, is Oxford College, founded in 1836 as a Methodist school. The birthplace of Emory University, it claims a number of ghosts, some from the Civil War.

Oxford's Civil War spooks stalk the halls of Phi Gamma Hall, the oldest structure on campus, constructed in 1851. The school closed in 1861 when faculty and students joined the Confederate military, but during the fighting around Atlanta, the buildings were utilized as hospitals. The dead were buried nearby at a site located today a short distance down a trail near the gym.

For decades, students have reported unexplained phenomena in Phi Gamma Hall, although that accelerated during a renovation. "Floors creak as if a person is walking across," a student publication claims. "Windows buckle and doors creak."

Michael Silverio saw lights turn on and off by themselves when the electricity was disconnected. Jared Van Aalten was plastering a wall late one night, and as the material dried, a particular area started to drip, leaving the image of a skull on the wall.

In October 2010, *Covington News* reporter Amber Pittman interviewed Dr. Joe Moon, dean of campus life at Oxford, asking about the ghosts of the school.

"This is where Sherman's troops marched through," he said. "Many of these buildings were used as hospitals and soldiers were brought here from Atlanta for treatment. When they died, they were carried down this path and buried."

The path is a nature trail that leads through woods to a Confederate cemetery. According to Moon, "You always hear about students seeing movement or feeling things or hearing screams down here. During the daytime, it's kind of nice, but at night, it's very spooky.

"It was here [Phi Gamma Hall] in the Civil War when all the death occurred and it does have a story," Moon continued. Facing the library entrance are several large windows. For years, it had been a study room closed at night. Many students leaving the library in the early evening swore they sighted a woman dressed in white, whom they called a nurse.

"They all described her as frantic, saying she seemed distraught and would pace back and forth in front of the windows," the dean said. The study room was closed for a few years before reopening as an attractive twenty-four-hour study area. Since the reopening, the "nurse" has not been reported.

Seney Hall, dating to 1881, has long been known for strange sounds. A former professor swore that late at night as he worked, he saw a ghost in his office.

"He described it as a young boy, about seventeen or eighteen, and he said that it reminded him of a Confederate soldier," Moon related. "He said the boy was not malicious and that he was never scared, but that he would sit there quietly and watch until the boy faded away."

Because the building was post Civil War, Moon doubted the ghost was Civil War related. He reconsidered that position when he learned the site was Main or Old Main, one of the original campus structures that had been used as a hospital. Materials from Old Main were used to construct Seney Hall.

Nearly every building on campus has been rumored to have been haunted, at least by thumps and movement when professors or staff members were alone in the building.

The Haunted Mill

Johnny Wells constructed Henderson Mill on the Alcovy River in the southeastern corner of Newton County during the early 1800s. The original mill was three stories tall, thirty feet wide and thirty-six feet deep, and after two rooms were added, it enclosed 5,200 square feet. Ray and Cindy Bryan, who spent eight years restoring the structure for use as their home, purchased the historic mill in 1976. Fortunately, they were able to keep various mill features, including a corn grinder and the bagger. The third floor, which is a huge loft, is haunted by a nine-year-old slave named Benjie. Ray related the story to Cindy Smith Brown for *Middle Georgia Magazine*.

When the Federal troops were in the area during the war, they set fire to a sawmill, wagon shop and cotton gin nearby. They also shelled the mill causing considerable smoke damage. Benjie, his nineteen-year-old sister, Mannie, and the mill's overseer went up to the third floor looking for safety. Fortunately, some of…Wheeler's boys [Confederate cavalry] came by and [ran] off the Yankees before the mill was burned down. Mannie and the overseer decided to drop Benjie out the third-floor window, hoping to save his life. But Benjie got twisted in the fall and died. The ghost tracers who've been here tell me Benjie's here with me all the time, and when things go missing, he's the one who takes them or moves them.

The mill is located off Georgia 36 at the intersection of Dixie Road and Henderson Mill Road.

WALTON COUNTY

When War Passed Through

According to the *Butler Herald* of June 2, 1885, a man, woman and child from Connecticut were trapped in Walton County by the war. They took up residence in an old house at High Shoals, on the Walton-Oconee county line along the Apalachee River, perhaps working in the High Shoals Manufacturing Company. After Sherman passed nearby, the man disappeared. The woman and child "professed ignorance of his whereabouts, and soon returned home." It was speculated that the man "had been foully dealt with, had been murdered by [Union] camp followers." According to the *Herald*, from that point on:

Every family which moved into the house as quickly moved out of it. The moving of a human being, accompanied by the clanking sound of chains, low moans of pain, and many mysterious sounds, would be heard. People traveling a distance could see lights at the windows, and on nearing them all would vanish. The most intelligent people soon began to look upon the place with horror, and no amount of money could induce them to sleep in the house over night. Travelers after night would go out of their way rather than pass the premises…

In the still hours of the night hundreds of reliable witnesses attest that they have been aroused from quiet slumber by the strangest and most unearthly sounds. In one room last week a mother was heard rocking her babe to sleep and singing a wee lullaby; the doors were thrown suddenly open and persons were heard walking up and down the stairs.

Some time since a prominent preacher who scoffed at the idea of ghosts, spent a night at this house. The next morning he appeared pale and haggard, and stated that he would not sleep another night beneath the roof for all the gold in the universe. Families have been known to pack up at midnight and leave rather than brave the terrors which seemed to stand between them and daylight, being driven off through fear at the strange sounds heard.

Madison

Legend has it that one of Madison's lovely antebellum homes was used as a Civil War hospital. Today, footsteps are heard on the stairs by night, and a tall man dressed in black appears at the top landing. A phantom ball bounces down a hallway, and in one room, a lady clad in an old fashioned blue dress materializes.

Eatonton: Sylvia and the Civil War

"Sylvia" was written by Louise Reid Pruden Hunt, former owner of Panola Hall, who frequently saw Sylvia:

Sylvia's coming down the stair—
Pretty Sylvia, young and fair.
Oft and oft, I meet her there,
Smile on lip and rose in hair.
Stand aside and let her pass—
Little room she takes, alas!
Sylvia died, they tell me so,
Died a hundred years ago.

Panola Hall had some bad decades, changing owners frequently and, at one point, becoming a boarding house. Preservationists feared it might be beyond repair when the structure was purchased in the mid-1990s by Rick Owens, who worked in an Atlanta hospital and worked on the house in his free time.

Owens was taken aback when the previous owner candidly admitted, "By the way, there's a ghost."

Owens pondered the situation before deciding, "I didn't know what to expect, but I didn't have a bad feeling about the place," he told *Atlanta Journal Constitution* reporter Bill Osinski in 1998.

The accounts he found of Sylvia described her as a bit haughty with those she judged her social inferiors but also as beautiful and laughing, her presence accompanied by the scent of roses.

After Owens had lived there for a few years, Sylvia decided at last to reveal herself to him.

"She was there just long enough for her presence to register with me. But it was so clear. I can still see her," Owens said.

The transparent apparition was a beautiful young woman attired in a ruffled blouse and waist length jacket. As usual, the girl appeared at the landing of the main stairs.

Owens's only problem with the situation was Halloween—up to three hundred kids descended on the one documented haunted house in the town of Eatonton.

Several times, Owens has entered the house to be greeted by the strong scent of freshly baked cinnamon buns.

A traditional version of Sylvia's story has her as a guest living in Panola Hall during the war. Hearing that her fiancé had been killed in battle, the young woman jumped off the balcony and died when she stuck the brick sidewalk.

———

The song "Marching Through Georgia" by Henry Clay Work was inspired by Sherman's March in 1865. The joyful marching song won wide appeal and the sheet music sold an unprecedented million copies.

> *Bring the good ol' bugle, boys we'll sing another song;*
> *Sing it with the spirit that will start the world along,*
> *Sing it like we used to sing it fifty thousand strong,*
> *While we were marching through Georgia.*

———

MILLEDGEVILLE

Marching Through Georgia's State Capital

In 1807, the capital of Georgia moved west with the growing state, from Louisville to Milledgeville. A capitol was constructed near the Oconee River, and despite fires and reconstructions, it is considered the oldest public building in the Gothic style existing in the United States.

The question of secession was vigorously debated in the legislative chamber before the ordinance was passed on January 19, 1861. A torchlight parade of excited citizens toured the streets. Those residents were considerably subdued four years later when Sherman concentrated his sixty-thousand-man army in and around Milledgeville. Governor Joseph Brown and a few troops—cavalry and militia—had just withdrawn without firing a shot.

Milledgeville was largely spared destruction as a provost guard was established on the Capitol grounds. However, raucous Union troops held a mock session of the state legislature that "repealed" the ordinance of secession. Afterward, they trashed the building and destroyed many official papers and the state library.

Ghostly Confederate sentries pace between Georgia's old Capitol and the governor's mansion in Milledgeville. Militaristic sounds echo across the old capital at night.

Georgia's capital moved to Atlanta in 1868. For several years, the old Capitol building served as the Baldwin County Courthouse but later became home to Middle Georgia Military and Agricultural College, which is now Georgia Military College (GMC).

Capitol Ghosts

This hulking Gothic castle looks haunted, and it is. A lone Confederate sentry has been spotted marching back and forth from the Capitol to the Governor's Mansion. Students at Vinson Hall have heard a ghostly bugler sounding "Taps," a tune that originated with a Union general in 1862 and was very probably played by Sherman's men in their camps ringing Milledgeville. People working late in the old Capitol have heard phantom footsteps following them through the legislative chamber. On quiet, dark nights, the sound of a large body of soldiers marching is heard in the streets, perhaps Sherman's confident veterans entering yet another conquered Confederate city.

When wind blows across the Gothic towers, a sound known locally as the "soul winds," eerie and shrill, is heard in the community, sounding like moaning, crying or the howling of wolves.

During a book signing of *Weird Georgia* at Barnes & Noble in Macon in 2006, I met Erin Evans, who submitted her account of a ghost sighting at the old Capitol. One night around 2:00 a.m., she and a friend were out walking around Milledgeville's quiet streets. As they neared the Capitol, "we noticed a young man walking along the edge of the building," she wrote. "The man was wearing a funny looking hat and half cape. When we got closer, he stopped walking and stared at us. Feeling uneasy, we turned to leave, I looked back, and the man was gone."

After describing the encounter to a friend who attended GMC, Erin was taken to the museum located inside the building and shown a Confederate uniform.

"To my shock, it was the exact uniform I had seen the night before on the mysterious man. My friend explained that other GMC students reported hearing shouting and seeing strange fog and a man walking around the old Capitol."

After reading a published account of a similar incident, Erin concluded, "I'm sure I saw that Confederate soldier that night, interrupting his nightly guard over the old Capitol."

The Haunted Executive Mansion

The beautiful Governor's Mansion in Milledgeville has witnessed a great deal of history. The Greek Revival house was completed in 1838 and hosted governors for thirty years. During the Civil War, it was occupied by Joseph Brown, one of the most difficult governors with whom the Confederate government had to contend. Brown had plenty of notice that Sherman was approaching and vacated the premises with all the furniture. His panic amused Sherman, who slept on the bare floor in the mansion. Perhaps it is the smoke from the general's cigars that are occasionally detected in the library.

For ten years after the capital was moved to Atlanta, the pink stucco structure was a boarding house, and it later served as a dorm for Georgia Military and Agricultural College. The building became a residence for presidents of Georgia College and is now preserved as a house museum. Its most prominent ghost is thought to be Molly, who spent her life cooking for governors and allegedly for Sherman as well. She manifests herself with the tantalizing smells of her cooking, particularly pork and black-eyed peas, which emanate from the long unused kitchen. Phantom footsteps are heard, doors open and close of their own accord and lights are switched on and off. When guests stayed, the housemaids would change the linens in one particular room only to return to find the covers wadded up in a corner. Several workers refused to enter that room.

In 1993, Georgia College student David Hibberts was writing his thesis about Molly. "One of the guests even found his bed turned down and no one had been there," he learned.

In October 1994, the exhumed remains of Ike Turner, a Confederate captain, lay in state for two days before being transported to his native Texas. Large numbers of people circulated through the mansion that weekend during a living history exercise, and when it was over, the grand mansion was permeated by the smell of burned potatoes. The fire department was summoned but found nothing amiss. Everyone concluded that the flood of visitors had so disturbed Molly that she allowed her food to burn. On another occasion in 1994, Georgia College students who were helping to cater a dinner were startled by the sudden appearance of a woman dressed in a long, dark dress with her hair secured in a bun. When the students spoke to her, the silent woman smiled, nodded and then vanished in an instant.

During the war, Georgia governor Joseph Brown lived at Georgia's executive mansion in Milledgeville. The Civil War–era cook is still working.

James C. Turner, curator of the mansion, says that the governor's young brother, John Brown, was mortally wounded in battle. After being transported to the house, he died in 1864. "From time to time, people have heard him groaning," he told Kathleen Walls in *Georgia's Ghostly Getaways*.

How the darkeys shouted when they heard the joyful sound!
How the turkeys gobbled which our commissary found!
How the sweet potatoes even started from the ground;
While we were marching through Georgia.

TWIGGS COUNTY

The Haunted Center of Georgia

There is a spot in the wilds of Twiggs County that is the geographic center of Georgia. Not far away are the historic Richland Church, little altered since its construction in 1811, and an attendant cemetery. Isolated today, the church was once near an old stage route from Savannah to Milledgeville. Constructed in 1845 by architect William Sessions in carpenter Greek Revival, a wooden rail still divides the pews into sections for men and women, and in the gallery are the original slat-backed benches. Although services ceased in 1911, the building is maintained, and people still have their weddings there. There are stories of organ music being played late at night and the moans of wounded Confederates. When one of Sherman's wings swept through the area, it saw service as a hospital.

Georgia Haunt Hunt Club member Brad Huffman visited the church at 9:30 p.m. on December 26, 1998, while visiting relatives in the area. He and a cousin had been observing the structure for three minutes when they "saw a yellow dot of light near the woods behind the church." It hovered four feet above the ground, shifted three feet and vanished. Within seconds, three additional lights and the original appeared, two of the newcomers a set. The lighted pair was eleven feet high and drifted around while the others blinked and wavered before they all disappeared. The cousin spotted three lights descending the front steps of the church and vanishing into the ground.

"We then heard a sound like someone walking through the leaves and we both got a feeling of impending doom," Brad wrote in his case file. The steps approached from behind, precipitating flight. As they drove off, Brad spotted a light inside the church that disappeared and was replaced by a second pair that shifted color from orange-yellow to orange-red.

Brad and a friend (the cousin had clucked out) returned at 10:45 p.m. and "felt a big presence." As happened before, several minutes after their arrival the light show started, its stars floating about. The men "both felt something evil" and then heard the footsteps. They drove a short distance but "could still hear the footsteps," even above the engine noise. As the sounds closed on them, they "heard a noise like metal clanging and [their] car seemed to run rough for a brief second." The set of eyes was eight feet away, and after noting a gravestone with a yellow glow, Brad saw it was only three feet away: "I then saw dozens of others, singles, right on the edge of the road, fanning in a strip maybe seven feet long."

The men sped away, feeling the presence for about three miles. Both were chilled by the experience.

Brad made a final visit at 2:20 p.m. on the afternoon of December 27. He found "the area around the church and graveyard much colder than anywhere else, even in the daylight." He also had "a feeling of someone else being there, like [he] was being observed."

STATESBORO

Hell No I Ain't Forgettin'

Southerners are often accused of refusing to forget the war. The office at the Statesboro-Bulloch County Chamber of Commerce at 102 South Main Street was once inhabited by a ghost with that very philosophy. The building was quiet from the time of its construction until the late 1990s, when the chamber had the audacity to hire an employee of the Northern persuasion named Adam. One morning, employee James Drinkard arrived at work and was soon reporting a curious incident to his boss, Peggy Chapman, president of the chamber.

"He said he was turning to leave and glimpsed what looked like a man standing on the stairs with an old military suit on," Chapman told Vanessa Jenkins of the *Statesboro Herald*.

This appearance marked the beginning of the haunting by an entity that named itself Charlie. On another morning, Chapman arrived early and noticed an unusual mess on Drinkard's work space. "James was really neat," Chapman said, "there was never any paper out of place on his desk. That morning I noticed that there was paper all over James's desk. I looked closely and saw the paper was wadded up with the name 'Charlie' spelled out across the desk."

From that moment on, the chamber's resident ghost was called Charlie, and he certainly seemed to identify himself as such. Also from that point on, Charlie became bolder. A message from Charlie next appeared in a piece of office machinery.

"One day we came in and saw a piece of paper with 'Yankee go home Yankee go home Charlie' all over the paper in the typewriter," Chapman said. "It filled the whole page—it looked like someone had just colored all over it."

Another chamber employee, Shelia Tillman, removed copies from a machine and saw that on the back of each page was the printed name "Charlie."

One night, Chapman and her husband were working late. "My husband saw someone peek his head around my office door," Chapman said. "My husband asked me who it was, and I said it must be Charlie. He said it was as clear as day that someone was peeking [his] head around the door to see who was in the office."

Yankee Adam departed years ago, and with him, Charlie also vanished. Neither has been sighted for over a decade. "We think he was a Confederate soldier who was upset that we had a Yankee working here," Chapman believes. However, Charlie's memory is fondly cherished, as Chapman said: "Every time someone new comes in and [the staff] tells [him] that story, the new employees are scared to go on the second floor."

Horse Thieves of Bulloch County

A Bulloch County history book tells the story of a man named Johnson who had been part of a horse-thieving gang in South Carolina during the war and moved to Georgia, presumably to escape his past. If that was his purpose, he failed, for his victims traced him to Bulloch County, pronounced him guilty and hanged him from a persimmon tree that grew where the Smith-Tillman Mortuary stood in the 1970s. The tree survived for decades, but no one was willing to eat its fruit. Many residents reported that on the darkest nights, Johnson's body was seen swaying from a limb of that tree.

JENKINS COUNTY

Georgia's Other Andersonville

To help relieve the overcrowding and deadly conditions at Andersonville, Confederate officials built Camp Lawton at Magnolia Springs, near Millen, where seven million gallons of pure water flows daily. It was the South's largest POW camp, intended to hold 40,000 men within its forty-three enclosed acres. The site was a resort compared to Andersonville, with plenty of good water and adequate food, but shelter was primitive.

The stockade was ringed by forty sentry boxes and earthworks that contained eleven cannons. The prison housed only 10,279 prisoners, and the 685 to 1,330 who died during the 113-day occupation were later reinterred at Beaufort National Cemetery in South Carolina. Sherman had hoped to liberate the captives, but Southerners had time to evacuate the POWs farther south. Finding only graves, Sherman angrily burned the prison and, for good measure, most of Millen. Sights at the prison left his men in a savage mood—they pillaged and burned with ever-increasing ferocity, which led to a number of atrocities, as Confederate cavalry and irregulars took to executing captured Federals in retaliation.

Wade Huffman is the assistant manager at Magnolia Springs. A native of Twiggs County, he formerly worked at Laura Walker State Park in the Okefenokee Swamp near Waycross and lives in a house on the grounds.

In October 2006, during a full moon, he "woke up about two in the morning in the back of [his] house," he told me. He continued: "There was an apparition standing at the end of my bed, a full bodied apparition, wearing an officer's uniform. It woke me out of a deep sleep, calling my name. I sat up and looked at it. I could tell it was a soldier's uniform, but I could not tell if it was Union or Confederate. It was a younger guy, probably a teenager, and I could see it as plain as day. I saw it for a split second, and it was gone. It was as real as it gets."

One day, Park Manager Bill Giles drove up to Huffman's house: "There is a porch that comes off my kitchen and I was in the back of the house and Bill saw me walk up and he said, 'Wade, you were just in the kitchen, weren't you?' I said, 'No, I was in the back of the house.' In the outside side of the window you can see a face, just a face, looking out at you. He [Giles] thought he was me. I've seen that face. I've driven up several times and seen it and thought, 'I'm not in the house.'" Huffman is not certain if the figure in the window is the same one that appeared in his bedroom.

Giles told his version of the event: "I was walking to his back door when I saw something that looked like a face looking out his window. He answered the door, and I asked him, 'Who else is here?' cause he had to come from the back of the house to answer the door, and he said, 'It was just me.'"

Giles once lived in the assistant manager's residence that is now occupied by Huffman and had his own experiences there. "My wife and I have a cat," Giles said, "and the cat would wake us up every now and then in the middle of the night screaming and hissing and such" for no accountable reason.

Huffman said that the primary prison cemetery was located near the railroad at Lawtonville but that "there is another graveyard somewhere here, we don't know the exact location…One thing I sit and ponder was my house sitting on top of [that] gravesite, which it could very well be."

Manager Giles confirmed that the location of camp cemeteries was not accurately recorded. One or two burial trenches were near the edge of the spring for prisoners who died in the prison hospital, and another one was located two thousand yards away by the railroad for those who died on the trains en route. After the war, the bodies were exhumed and buried near the railroad at Lawton National Cemetery, which was only in existence for a few years. Eventually, 685 bodies were removed to Beaufort. A prisoner who kept the death book said a total of 1,330 men died, so there is a discrepancy of 645 bodies. "They might have missed a burial trench," Giles proposed.

"As many thousands of prisoners as were here, there's ghosts, whatever still exists after death," Huffman said. "If it is a spirit, it's going to be disturbed, because this was not a good life.

He continued: "You can be out there at night, and you feel like someone is following you, or you feel something rustling in the leaves, and it's not a deer

This spring supplied water to ten thousand Union prisoners at Magnolia Springs. One Civil War officer made a full body appearance at the bedside of an employee.

or anything like that; it sounds heavier. You get that strange feeling. I think it's just because the spirits are curious."

Although most of the deceased prisoners were disinterred long ago, "For the rest of them, who knows? It's interesting," Huffman said.

Despite the weirdness, he does not fear living there. "All park rangers have to like living isolated by themselves, like a hermit. It has never bothered me, because they haven't tried to do me any harm."

There are two haunted sites in Jenkins County. Magnolia Springs is a state park where the prison site remains, highlighted by Civil War earthworks. There are also camping facilities and cabins. Birdsville plantation near Millen was one of Georgia's finest when Sherman spent several days there in November 1864, while the mistress was mourning the recent death of a child. Perhaps it is that baby that cries at night and makes doors spontaneously open and close.

EFFINGHAM COUNTY

The Desperate Spirits of Ebenezer Swamp

In *To the Sea*, my book about William Sherman's infamous march from Atlanta to Savannah in the fall of 1864, I noted that the Union march was easy, resistance slight and morale high until after they passed east of Milledgeville. Then the winter rains commenced, heavy and cold, turning the best roads into quagmires and sickening the marching infantry. The bounty of the great plantations disappeared in the piney woods, and hunger became a constant companion. Escaped prisoners from Andersonville, mere living skeletons, stumbled into Union lines, enraging every man in Sherman's force. Finally, Confederate troopers, no longer having to defend Macon and a little later freed from protecting Augusta, were able to concentrate their attention against the Federals. There was no chance of stopping the Federal juggernaut, but the angry Southerners were constantly picking up stragglers and striking foraging parties. Things were getting ugly.

The fact that Abraham Lincoln had issued the Emancipation Proclamation did not make all Union soldiers abolitionists. Racists abounded in this army, both enlisted men and officers, and many of the "contrabands" were treated badly by their liberators. One of the worst racists under Sherman was a general with the unlikely name of Jefferson Davis, who always included his middle initial, C, to distinguish himself from the Confederate president.

Sherman himself instructed slaves to remain on their plantations. Liberty would come with victory, he argued. The hordes of slaves could not be fed and would present a serious liability if a battle developed.

Sherman's army crossed Georgia along four avenues of march. The most trying route was the one farthest north, through the swamps bordering the Savannah River. Numerous streams swelled to flood level, all but submerging the single road. Jeff Davis's fourteen-thousand-man division brought up the rear. The soldiers—exhausted, hungry, wet and cold—often had to heave heavy wagons and artillery pieces through the morass as rain continued to fall heavily. Donkeys disappeared into the mud (admittedly, *small* donkeys). Big naval cannons from Confederate ships on the Savannah rained shells onto the column. Then came reports that Confederate general Joseph Wheeler's cavalry was in the rear, pressing relentlessly.

When Davis came to Ebenezer Creek, he found the water swift, deep and one hundred yards wide. He ordered engineers to rig a pontoon bridge and posted armed guards to prevent any escaped slaves from passing before his entire division was across. The crowd of blacks increased steadily and apprehension grew at the sounds of combat from the rear. If seized by Confederates, they would be returned to their owners and probably punished severely. A few might be killed as examples.

As the Union rear guard crossed the bridge, Davis cut the span loose from the western bank, swinging it against the eastern shore. The fugitive slaves were horrified by the realization that their saviors had abandoned them. Hundreds pressed forward, plunging into the floodwaters or being pushed from behind. Men and women, many with babies in their arms, floundered in the swift current and were rapidly swept away.

A few Federals turned back and did what they could, felling big trees into the stream and heaving logs into the water, but they were forced to rejoin the column or be abandoned deep in enemy territory. They turned their eyes away, but the sounds beat at their ears—screaming, crying, pleading and doubtlessly cursing from the desperate souls that had been betrayed. The last they glimpsed of the hellish scene was a giant black man who desperately pulled a little raft repeatedly across the creek, saving all he could.

Most of the contrabands were returned to slavery, but unknown hundreds perished—the true number will never be known. It was the greatest loss of life on Sherman's grand march. An inquiry was urged by some, but nothing came of it. No one cared much about the fate of fugitive slaves.

The Savannah River swamps remain dangerous and forbidding. Many modern residents report that when the rains come day after dark day in the late fall and early winter and the streams overflow, they can still hear the mournful pleading and screams of the damned souls that were condemned in the swamps that day in 1864.

Yes and there were Union men who wept with joyful tears,
When they saw the honored flag they had not seen for years;
Hardly could they be restrained from breaking forth in cheers,
While we were marching through Georgia.

GUYTON

Vocal Ghosts

A Confederate military hospital operated at Guyton in Effingham County, and the dead were buried amid the good local citizens. There they lie in the center of the community cemetery, each grave indicated by blank markers—none are identified. On the night of May 11, 2006, DizzyGirl and her husband entered the grounds for a little ghost hunting, which they do occasionally. She sat in the Confederate section for fifteen minutes, saying aloud, "Is there anyone here who would like to communicate? Can you tell me your name?" and "Can you show me a sign that you're here?" She felt no response and moved to other areas of the cemetery. In the car on the way home, she replayed the tape and heard the whispered words, "This is Confederate." She wrote, "Every hair rose up on my skin."

FORT MCALLISTER

Fighting Ghosts

Savannah was vulnerable to approach from the Atlantic Ocean via a number of waterways. One of the most important was the Ogeechee River, a valuable shelter for blockade runners. To protect this route, the river was obstructed by Fort McAllister, a nine-gun earthen fort designed and constructed by Captain John McCready. Major John B. Gallie commanded the garrison of two hundred when the Union navy decided to destroy the position. On January 27, 1863, the ironclad monitor *Montauk*, accompanied by several wooden ships, steamed upriver and unleashed a five-hour bombardment. Despite the damage caused by sixty-one fifteen-inch, 450-pound explosive shells, the fort survived. At night, the garrison swarmed over the dirt and sand walls, easily repairing gaping holes.

The *Montauk* returned on February 1 and took position less than one thousand yards away. Throughout the bombardment Major Gallie ventured from one gun position to another, encouraging his gunners during the frightening attack. He chose as his personal position an eight-inch Columbiad because it was closest to the attackers. It and a thirty-two-pounder rifled cannon were the only pieces that could reach the *Montauk*, and in turn, the monitor concentrated its fire on those guns. A shell fragment wounded Gallie in the head, but he refused to go to the safety of a bombproof. The earthworks protecting his weapon were chewed to pieces, but the piece continued to fire, even when a Union fifteen-inch shell decapitated the major. Again Fort McAllister survived, and that night, the men repaired the massive destruction to the fort.

One month later, March 3, 1863, the Union navy returned, determined to subdue the stubborn Confederate fortification. Three ironclads came this time—*Passaic, Nahant* and *Patapsco*—accompanied by three mortar schooners and two wooden gunboats. The attack lasted seven hours, but McAllister suffered only one casualty: Tom Cat, the garrison's black cat mascot, killed while racing across the parapets. The animal, deeply mourned by the garrison, was mentioned in the official report of the battle. He was buried within the fort and is today commemorated by a historical marker.

The lack of results forced the Union navy to abandon its plan for reducing Fort McAllister. Nearly two years passed before William T. Sherman reached Savannah with his sixty-thousand-man army. He surrounded the city but needed to eliminate Fort McAllister to allow resupply and support

Confederate major Gallie was killed at his post during a Union bombardment of Fort McAllister. His headless apparition has been seen here.

by naval ships waiting offshore. On December 13, 1864, Sherman sent four thousand infantrymen against the fort's two hundred defenders. The Union advance was magnificent in the face of the opposing artillery, but the defenders covered themselves with glory. They fought furiously until Union forces smothered the fort and every Confederate was individually subdued. Sherman, observing nearby, called it "the handsomest thing I have seen in the war." Many Confederate and Union soldiers died in the brief battle.

Roger Durham, former director of Fort McAllister, never saw a ghost, but confided, "There are stories." When Henry Ford purchased a nearby plantation and had the fortification reconstructed during the 1930s, he asked workers to sleep on the grounds at night to prevent vandalism and theft of historic artifacts.

"Well, they never did spend a full night here!" Durham told Margaret DeBolt, author of *Savannah Spectres and Other Strange Tales*. "Sometime during the first night they were gone, and after that they were out of here every day at sundown. There were stories that they had heard strange sounds and so forth." He added, "Let's just say that it gets very dark and very quiet out there on the earthworks at night."

One February in the 1960s, park employees were working in the fort, cutting grass and doing general upkeep, when they noticed an abrupt, eerie silence accompanied by a sudden chilling sensation. Looking toward the remounted eight-inch Columbiad at Major Gallie's position, they spotted a headless man hovering above the earthworks. The apparition was clad in a blue militia uniform marked on the sleeves with officer's braid. After facing (figuratively, of course) the river for several minutes, it disappeared. The incident occurred at the same time on the anniversary of the day that Gallie died.

In *Ghost Stories of Georgia*, Chris Wangler tells of a North Carolina man who visited Fort McAllister in 2002. Hearing shouting, he thought a child was being disciplined but then realized that what he heard was a male voice shouting instructions to an artillery crew, culminating in the command, "Fire!" As he approached the Columbiad, he saw a hazy image of a man wearing an officer's uniform crouched at the artillery piece. As he walked forward, the apparition disappeared. Enquiring at the museum, the witness was told the story of Major Gallie.

A man with the Internet name Georgia Rebel snapped a number of photos around Fort McAllister, hoping something strange would register.

In December 1864, thousands of Union troops overwhelmed Fort McAllister, but some of its faithful defenders, and the garrison cat, remain in spirit.

His most unusual picture was taken inside the restored bombproof, where at one point, his camera malfunctioned. In the hospital portion of the facility, a ghostly figure is framed between two timbers. A careful examination shows what looks like the face, shoulders, trunk and legs of a man with a cartridge box at his waist.

The Confederate Cheshire Cat

Gallie may be McAllister's only human ghost, but there is also the phantom feline. A black cat has been seen by many visitors, usually running atop the earthworks, occasionally pausing to study the river. A number of reenactors have seen the whole cat or, sometimes, just the face or a tail disappearing behind earthworks. Some have felt a furry little ghost rubbing against their legs. It seems that Tom Cat has also not abandoned his post, or simply has not yet used up his remaining eight lives.

Chris Wangler also described the field trip of a young girl, Jessica Miller, a fifth grader from Atlanta in the 1980s. Ditching her group, Jessica scrambled up the earthworks that protected the Columbiad. There she was startled by the purring of an invisible cat. While hiding from a classmate, she continued to hear the ghost feline, which gave her a feeling of calm.

"Sherman's dashing Yankee boys will never make the coast!"
So the saucy Rebels said and 'twas a handsome boast;
Had they not forgot, alas! To reckon with the host,
While we were marching through Georgia.

LIBERTY COUNTY

South of Savannah, Confederate cavalry roamed Liberty County to watch for Union landings from the Atlantic Ocean. When Sherman besieged

A New England–style church stands in Midway. Confederate and Federal spirits fight in the cemetery across the highway.

and occupied Savannah, Federal cavalry scoured the county for food and terrorized its occupants.

Midway, a Colonial village dating from the 1700s, is well known for its historic, New England–style church and the walled cemetery across the road. Midway Cemetery boasts many ghosts, but in the back southwestern corner are two graves placed close together. One is occupied by a Confederate, the other by a Federal. According to Don Farrant in *Ghosts of the Georgia Coast*, local residents have seen the two warriors sitting on the ground quietly playing cards. However, the friendly game always ends in a fight as the two former enemies grapple angrily.

Just Passing Through

Farrant also described the haunting of a new house in Liberty County. In 1999, soon after the house was constructed, owner Meg Conover spotted a Native American, clad only in a loincloth, sitting in a chair. The ghost vanished, only to reappear several times to Meg and her husband, Jim, as it stalked through the house, sometimes staring back at them. On every appearance their three dogs growled and barked loudly.

Later, a second entity entered their residence, announced by their pets, which stared at the back door like watchdogs. When they started barking, a series of loud raps were made on the outside of the door. Meg thought the rapping was a signal for the dogs to stop barking, and indeed, "They immediately quieted down."

Several days later, Meg and Jim were sitting in their living room when an apparently solid human being walked out of the kitchen into the living room and entered a guest room. The figure was dressed in a gray Confederate officer's uniform with a stiff collar, two rows of buttons in the front, a tasseled, knotted sash at his waist, high cavalry boots and a hat with insignia. He looked at the couple and continued on his journey. The apparition has repeatedly visited the Conovers, who consider him a friendly spirit and call him the Colonel.

Three Maids All in a Row

Hinesville is located in an area that Sherman never reached, but his foragers roamed the area destroying property, seizing foodstuffs and frightening residents. Reportedly a father, driven insane by reports that marauding Federals were approaching, chopped off the heads of his three daughters and threw them in a well. For nearly a century and a half, the girls have been seen wandering the area looking (psychically, we assume) for their noggins.

Several additional Civil War–related hauntings occurred farther down the coast.

JEKYLL ISLAND

The Wealthy Confederate Ghosts

The Jekyll Island Club was founded in 1886 by such financial tycoons as Rockefeller, Vanderbilt, Pulitzer and J.P. Morgan. A complex of luxurious homes was constructed between 1887 and 1902. Jekyll Island was often the economic center of the world until World War II, when it was feared that America's elite would be killed or kidnapped by a Nazi U-boat raid. Georgia purchased the property in 1947, and the elegant Jekyll Island Club opened to the public in 1988.

Lloyd Aspenwald was the first president of the Jekyll Island Club, but unfortunately, he died, before the club was completed, on September 4. A room in the hotel was named for him, and employee Sue Anderson said that on each September 4, he appears in that room and strolls along the veranda. On these occurrences, Aspenwald is often seen wearing his old Confederate uniform.

Another Confederate spirit there is Samuel Spencer, an engineer and president of the Southern Railroad, who occupied Apartment Eight. He died in 1906 in, ironically, a train collision. Spencer loved a cup of coffee with his morning paper, and modern guests find their newspapers rearranged and coffee moved or even consumed.

GOLDEN ISLES

The Original Evil Eye

A persistent ghost story among the Gullah who still inhabit Georgia's Golden Isles is the plat eye, an evil spirit with only one eye that dangled from the center of its face. This entity was a slave killed, and often beheaded, by plantation owners and denied a proper burial so that he or she could act as guardian over treasure buried deep in swamps or woods, placed there to evade Sherman's bummers or raids from Union ships.

So we made a thoroughfare for Freedom and her train,
Sixty miles of latitude, three hundred to the main;
Treason fled before us, for resistance was in vain
While we were marching through Georgia.

PART II
SAVANNAH'S CIVIL WAR SPECTERS

S avannah is one of America's oldest cities, founded in 1733, and a strategic port. Mere months after the start of the war, an effective Union blockade denied Savannah's use to the Confederacy. Extensive earthen fortifications armed with huge cannons and three ironclads were constructed to deter a Federal assault, and historic Savannah survived until late 1864, when William T. Sherman's powerful army arrived and forced its evacuation. Savannah, a thoroughly haunted community, retains numerous ghosts from Civil War battles, enemy occupation and military hospitals and prisons.

FORT PULASKI

That fine Savannah writer Margaret DeBolt collected several Fort Pulaski stories for her definitive work, *Savannah Specters*. An employee at the fort denies personally experiencing any unusual events but confided that "one of the fellows here absolutely refuses to go into what [they] still call Colonel Olmstead's quarters, after dark."

Colonel Charles H. Olmstead, commander of Fort Pulaski, occupied one of the rooms constructed inside the casemates. He did not die at Fort Pulaski but was forced to surrender the post, certainly the equivalent of death for a professional soldier. The official capitulation occurred in Olmstead's quarters.

A Looter's Redemption

A truly strange experience deeply affected a soldier intent on looting artifacts from the grounds surrounding Fort Pulaski. He and a friend, both stationed at Hunter Army Airfield, were on leave one weekend when they decided to row a boat from Tybee Island to Cockspur Island. On a quiet, bright, still night, they took a metal detector and landed near the fort. They were walking through tall marsh grass toward the fort when "all at once it sounded like someone else was there, on the other side of a clump of bushes," he said. "This surprised me, as I had thought we were the only ones there."

His friend heard the noise, too. The startled men stopped, and a moment later, so did the shadow walker. The pair started forward again, and so did their unseen companion, the stride long and heavy, "like a man's," and traveling in the same direction. When the bushes ended, they expected to encounter the other intruder, "Only we couldn't see anything! As we stood there, we could watch the tall grass mash down, as though someone were walking right in front of us, then past us, and on out into the marsh."

Without a word the men simultaneously turned and sprinted for the boat, rowing across the water in record time.

The experience had a profound impact on the young man. After he left the service, he earned a college degree in history and became director of a Savannah area–historic site. Why? Because of his feeling "of completely belonging, of having been there before."

There was a hint of reincarnation in the account, a feeling he only felt elsewhere at Gettysburg.

The man accompanied DeBolt to Fort Pulaski, although he felt "an overpowering sense of sadness from the past" and had avoided visiting it until then. He must have been somewhat psychic, for he dreaded going into the casemate used as a prison for Confederate officers. He did not feel "an actual presence" but an "overwhelming sense of absolute misery, despair, and death."

He also had bad feelings about one stairway where he felt "great suffering, and someone probably died there." A park ranger believed that those stairs were used to carry a dying soldier down from the ramparts.

Still on Duty

During World War II, a woman was returning to Savannah from Tybee Island when she glanced at the fort and clearly saw "a number of men in some type of uniform walking about on top of the walls." She and a soldier companion observed them for several minutes.

It seems that the Confederate garrison at Fort Pulaski was determined to solider on. In *Battlefield Ghosts*, B. Keith Toney tells the story of a mother and her boy who were intrigued by a Confederate sentry at the moat gate one day. They asked him about the authentic looking uniform and sword, and then the mother requested the location of the restrooms. The sentry replied that he would show them but could not leave his post. The mother thanked him and entered the fort.

Inside, she encountered a ranger and asked him about the facilities. When he replied that they were near the entrance, she was irritated and described her encounter with the sentry. "There's no one on duty over there," the park employee replied. "We don't have soldiers dressed in Confederate uniforms at the fort."

Fort Pulaski is one of the most haunted forts in America—phantom sentries have been seen on duty atop its walls.

Author James Caskey is a reenactor. During the holidays in 2002, reenactors and their period-dressed ladies enjoyed ginger cookies and cider in front of a blazing fire in the soldiers' quarters. While singing traditional Christmas songs, James suddenly fell ill. "I experienced a claustrophobic despair unlike any I've ever felt," he wrote in *Haunted Savannah*. "My whole body began tingling, and I had to step outside."

An older reenactor followed to see if he was okay. James explained that he had never felt that way, prompting the elder man to reply, "You're not the first. Given the history of that area you were just standing, it isn't a shock at all. It happens all the time—people feel sick, and once they get outside they feel fine."

Caskey described one couple who spotted a uniformed sentry on the parapet at sundown. "He was standing at the edge," the woman stated, "wearing a dark blue jacket, and then he simply stepped back out of view. I walked back, to get a better view of him, but he was gone." Her reenactor husband believed the figure was wearing a dark Confederate color known as Richmond Gray.

Caskey heard of a man touring a powder magazine at Fort Pulaski when he heard from a disembodied voice: "I distinctly heard someone say, 'Charlie, come here'…and no one was there," the man said. "It sounded like he was right there at my shoulder when he spoke, but I could see no one around me."

Mine Eyes Have Seen Glory

Hundreds of reenactors participated in filming *Glory*, the movie about the black Fifty-fourth Massachusetts Regiment that was shot around Savannah. During a break, nine men dressed in Confederate uniforms decided to visit Fort Pulaski. Outside the wall, probably inspecting the massive damage inflicted by Union artillery, they came upon a young man sharply dressed as a Confederate lieutenant. They nodded at their presumed fellow reenactor and continued on their way.

"Halt!" the lieutenant shouted, according to Toney. "Don't you men salute a superior officer when you see one?"

A few of the mock Confederates returned a half-hearted salute, several just shrugged and one was in no mood to play along, growling, "We ain't on the set yet!"

The officer stalked forward and said, "Sir, I don't know to what you are referring, and frankly don't care! Your insolence, however, will be noted and not tolerated. Now, fall in! Colonel Olmstead has recalled all work parties. The Yankee attack is imminent."

The men looked at each other and decided that this might be a show for the tourists. They formed a line and when the young officer barked, "Attention! About face!" they complied smartly. The next instruction should have been "Forward! March!" but it never came. When the reenactors looked back, the lieutenant had vanished.

"We searched all around the place," one said. "Never found any trace of him. We kept an eye out around the movie set, too. Never saw him there, either. Hard as it is to believe, we've all pretty much accepted he was a ghost. If he wasn't, we'd sure like to hear from him—that was one good-looking uniform he had on."

The Immortal One

The long Union siege of Charleston produced several vengeful acts. In retaliation for Federal shelling of the city, Confederate authorities placed 600 Union officer POWs in the threatened areas. In response, Federal officials placed 600 Confederate officer POWs on Sullivan's Island, in the line of Southern artillery fire. When this farce had played out, 550 of the Confederate officers were taken to Fort Pulaski, arriving on October 23, 1864, and placed in a barred section of casemates. Poorly fed and sheltered, many developed scurvy and dysentery. The 13 who died were buried outside the fort on Cockspur Island. The officers became famous in Southern lore as the Immortal 600.

A group of Confederate reenactors placed a laurel wreath at the graves on March 18, 1994, and then settled down inside the fort for the night. Later a twelve-year-old boy named Nicholas snuck out and walked around the perimeter of the fort, a quiet area cooled by ocean breezes. Nearing the graves, he spotted a figure in Confederate uniform with prominent gold scroll braiding decorating the sleeves on his knees beside the graves, his hat respectfully removed and held in hand. Nicholas did not recognize the man, who stood, started walking away and faded into nothing.

The frenzied lad raced into the fort and reported the incident. All the reenactors were present—none had ventured outside the walls. The group decided that one of the Immortal 600 had returned to pay homage to his comrades.

Run Away

In January 2001, on a cold, rainy night, Fox Family filmed a segment of the *Scariest Places on Earth* TV show within "Haunted Fort Pulaski" with the assistance of Bobbie Weyl, who is a local psychic, and three history students from Armstrong-Atlantic State University. The camera team was spooked by unexplainable sounds within the brick casemates, and camera batteries quickly lost their charge.

During the assignment, Weyl felt great despair and agony on a parapet and on the stairs leading to where a Confederate soldier was mortally wounded. She also sensed the presence of soldiers and supply wagons on the parade grounds. The college students were to spend the night within the fortification, but the sight of a spectral sentry pacing the parade ground and the sounds of shutting doors and footfalls both behind and in front of them led to their hasty departure at three in the morning.

Foundation for Paranormal Research members John and Julie Williams became interested in the paranormal when they were Civil War reenactors ten years ago. While in a room at Fort Pulaski, they both witnessed two doors open and close by themselves. "The doors opened in different directions so I could not explain it away," Julie explained. On another occasion, a cold night when Julie was sleeping in a room filled with other women, she wished to herself that it had been warmer. Immediately, a dying fire roared back to life. "I was immediately scared," Julie admitted. "I didn't know they could read your mind. It's cool when something happens, but I'm relieved when it doesn't."

On July 3, 2005, DizzyGirl posted an account on Ghost Hounds of expeditions to Fort Pulaski:

> *There's one room, the dark confinement room where they kept prisoners, that really sparked my interest. The room in question had no lights on during one of our visits, so I had stepped inside to take a flash pic. That way I could see what was in the room when we got home. When I stepped into the room, I felt like something was sitting on my chest. I felt threatened, and I just couldn't get out of the room quick enough. When we got home, we saw a few 'orbs,' but chalked it up to an overactive imagination or dust in the air.*
>
> *Well, in March my family came to visit, and we took them to the fort. I was telling my family about my experience with the room, and they asked to have their picture taken in it…One is of my mother, sister and brother-in-*

law. My sister was joking about having a ghost sit on her hand. The size of the orb above her is amazing.

The second photo really shocked me. As I was snapping the photo, my mother, a devout Catholic woman I might add, was saying a small prayer and asking whatever it was in the room, if anything, to move on or to show itself. It frightened me when she did it, because I don't like the thought of inviting anything, so you can imagine my shock when I got home and saw how bright that sucker was.

In August 2004, Jason Thomason related on ghostvillage.com that on his third trip to Fort Pulaski, he concentrated on the concrete storage tunnels (which he heard had sometimes held prisoners or escaped slaves) located beneath earthen mounds on the grounds. "Just entering the rooms sent chills up my spine," he wrote and, seeing an orb on his display screen, immediately snapped a digital shot. After downloading the pictures onto his computer, "I was surprised to find the first orb appeared to have a face, along with more orbs in some of the other areas, and perhaps even something more eerie, what appears to be a face on the wall of a guard's room." As on every trip to the fort, he "definitely felt something, or someone, in this place."

Chris Wangler, in *Ghost Stories of Georgia*, tells of a vacationing Atlantan who in 1965 rowed from Tybee Island to Cockspur Island to engage in his hobby: bird watching. Near the exterior wall of Fort Pulaski, he spotted a piece of gauze stained with blood. The call of a bird distracted the naturalist for a moment, and when he returned his gaze to the ground, the gauze had vanished. He did find what he concluded was a dried bloodstain on the brick wall itself.

The Phantom Lassie

Ghost Hound member Pam was visiting Fort Pulaski, peering into a room within the fort, when she "felt the unmistakable feeling of a dog's nose in my palm, the way a dog will nose into your hand looking for reassurance." She believes "that there is the spirit of a dog that's still there, and [it] wanted to say 'hi.' It was a very friendly kind of nose-touch."

FORT JACKSON

Fort Jackson, far upstream of Fort Pulaski on the Savannah River, not far from the port facilities, is Savannah's oldest surviving fortification. Although no battle was fought there, it was headquarters for the city defenses, and the men who were stationed there certainly left their psychic imprint.

The most dramatic story involves a Private Patrick Garrity, a guard once stationed at the entrance spanning the moat. One night, three officers had been sitting outside the walls socializing. When one of them, a Lieutenant George Dickinson, walked past the private over the drawbridge to enter the fort, Garrity snapped. He aimed his rifle at the officer's back and pulled the trigger, but the piece misfired. Garrity quickly reversed his rifle, grabbing it by the barrel and clubbing the officer over the head four times, repeatedly fracturing his skull. Seeming to realize what he had done, the private dove into the moat and drowned, his motive forever a mystery. The officer survived without memory of the attack or its cause. A number of visitors have noted the ghost of the crazed soldier, eternally on guard for his criminal act.

Each year, a deserving reenactor is presented with the "Garrity Award," shaped like a Civil War musket. The first year it was presented, a piece

Fort Jackson's Civil War sentry is still seen at his post, where he assaulted an officer before drowning himself in the moat.

of it disappeared and "was later found on the drawbridge," attendant Daniel Grisette told Kathleen Walls. "The following year, a different piece of the musket was mysteriously broken off. It, too, was later found on the drawbridge."

Savannah author James Mack Adams has heard several stories of Fort Jackson's spooks. He described a young cleaning woman on her first day of employment. She was inside the fort working after the facility had closed and heard a noise. Turning, she saw "a figure dressed in a Confederate uniform" at an open door. After a few seconds, the phantom turned and walked away. The employee went home and never returned, phoning in her resignation the next morning.

A former site manager told Adams that one night, he observed "a shadowy figure" walking across the parade ground. Thinking it was a friend, he called his name, but the apparition did not reply. Upon reaching the center of the parade ground, the figure "suddenly vanished." The character, clad in a long gray frock cloak, was invisible from the waist down.

Site manager Greg Starbuck admitted that ghostly soldiers were not uncommon at Fort Jackson, which gets very dark amid the marshes at night. He said workers will get "an eerie feeling" and then, spotting a mysterious form that seems to wear Civil War–era military clothing, think it "is one of [his] employees…and then they will realize they are the last person at the site" and suddenly understand "this is not one of their co-workers."

SAVANNAH

Sherman's Haunted Headquarters

General Sherman's Savannah headquarters might not have been haunted when he was a guest, but it certainly is now. The Green-Meldrim House, or St. John's Episcopal Rectory (14 West Macon Street), is a magnificent Gothic Revival structure designed by architect John S. Norris of New York City. It was constructed by Charles Green, who made a fortune in cotton and shipping, at a cost of $93,000 (over $4 million today). Green kindly allowed Sherman to use his home in December 1864, and the general and his staff enjoyed a fine Christmas dinner there.

Edward M. Green inherited the house in 1881, and eleven years later, it was sold to Judge Peter W. Meldrim. In 1943 St. John's Episcopal Church

Union general William T. Sherman made his Savannah headquarters at the Green-Meldrim House, which retains the ghost of a former servant.

purchased the house for use as a rectory. The first minister to live there was Reverend Ernest Risley, who often played the piano and harpsichord and played classical music on his phonograph. Reverend Risley witnessed the first ghostly activity in the building. When he was alone, one door would always open from no discernible cause.

In the 1990s, Reverend William H. Ralston Jr. stated his belief that the responsible party was Judge Meldrim's servant, Joe, who loved the parties his employer hosted, particularly the music. He nearly danced as he distributed refreshments to the guests. Reverend Ralston heard Joe's footsteps as the servant walked from room to room in his eternal duties and playfully tugged on women's purses while they toured the historic mansion.

The General's Annoying Children

Samuel P. Hamilton, a Confederate major general and Savannah mayor, constructed the Hamilton-Turner House (330 Hamilton-Abercorn Street, 1892), now a bed-and-breakfast. Nancy Hillis owned the ten-thousand-square-foot, four-story structure from 1991 until 1997 and converted it into an inn. She told Shelia Turnage, author of *Haunted Inns of the Southeast*, that during renovations, she and a tenant often heard children giggling from the empty top floor, and a friend heard the merriment and "Daddy" being playfully repeated. Several guests have heard the chant "Mom-Mom-Mom."

Hamilton had five mischievous children whose room occupied the top floor. One night, their behavior had gotten them banned from one of their father's frequent and popular parties. Angry, they careened billiard balls down the staircase, hitting a guest in the head, which caused a wound requiring several stitches to close. After a tour guide in the house heard the billiard balls one day, she refused to return. Others have registered the breaking of pool balls and laughter, and a former renter said the general (literally) passed through the house all the time.

General Hamilton's often-seen ghost has been described as "a milky cast in the form of a man," standing at the top of the stairs, Hillis said, and one night, she heard a heavy person running up those stairs. Police were summoned, but no one was found; the outside doors were all locked from the inside. Several guests have reported the presence of a man having a heart attack, which is what killed General Hamilton.

Walking Down Your Streets

At least two Confederate soldiers have been spotted roaming the streets of Savannah. Perhaps a casualty from one of the military hospitals organized in the city, one figure in a faded Confederate uniform has been sighted repeatedly in a home at the intersection of Gordon and Lincoln Streets, according to Margaret DeBolt in *Savannah Specters*. Another Confederate has also been seen in an 1850 house on East Jones Street near Bull Street.

After serving in the Confederate military, a number of Southern men wore gray, uniform-like suits for the remainder of their lives. In the following decades, stories of ghosts clad in gray became common. On August 13, 1944, the *Savannah Morning News* related the following story:

> *In one of the old Savannah homes of a generation ago there had dwelt for many, many years a group of spirits. The children of the house were taught to accept these kindly spirits as a matter of course. They saw them occasionally, especially on winter evenings. There was a special one the*

children spoke of as the Little Gray Man. He often ascended the stairs, and once one of the girls, although she never liked particularly to pass him, trailed up after him. He continued to the garret and disappeared into the big brick chimney, although there was no opening.

Unfortunately, after three generations, the house passed out of family ownership, but the stories survived for many years. The newspaper continued the story:

The granddaughters are now grandmothers, but they remember quite well the Little Gray Man and his associates. It was not an unusual occurrence when company was present and the grown folk sat in the living room, that all present would hear the sound of footsteps coming up the steps and crossing the porch.

Savannah was more quiet then than now, the streets were not paved, and a village silence prevailed. The company would cease talking and glance expectantly toward the door, only to be assured by the lady of the house that there was no one there. And it always turned out she was right though the front door would not be opened, the footsteps could be heard as the spirits continued down to the hall, or up the stairs.

On one occasion when the family was going for a ride in the phaeton the mother sent one of the little girls back to get her shawl which she had left on the back of a chair. The little girl came back empty handed, explaining that the Little Gray Man was sitting on it. She was sent back with orders to speak politely to him, and soon she reappeared with the shawl for her mother.

In summary, the Little Gray Man "warmed at the hearth during the chilly evenings, then came and went with perfect freedom, used the chairs at times, but did no harm."

A house located a block from Broughton Street was haunted by a Confederate officer, known to the house's living occupants as "the man in gray." Visitors spotted a vague shape strolling the halls and gardens and heard unaccountable noises. The gracious Southern lady of the house treated the officer as she would any ordinary visitor. She spoke kindly as they passed in the halls and spent many afternoons sewing in his presence.

Other men dressed in gray have been sighted in Savannah but are not demonstrable Civil War soldiers. Gray ghosts are a common phenomenon.

The Haunted Hotel

During the summer of 1999, Kathleen Thomas, features editor for *Creative Loafing: Savannah*, was preparing an article about the Marshall House at 123 East Broughton Street, which was about to open as a fine hotel. As founder of the Searchers, a ghost hunting organization, she asked the general manager, director of sales and administrative assistant if they had experienced any paranormal activity. All three had heard doors slammed and heavy things dropped in the upper stories when they were alone in the building. Management eagerly accepted an offer by the Searchers to investigate the situation.

On the night of July 31, a diverse army of twenty Searchers descended on the establishment with five 35 mm cameras, two video cameras and two digital cameras, all devices that would allow them to record ghostly figures and other phenomena that are manifested visually. They also brought three tape recorders to capture audio expressions (often emitted below human hearing), three digital thermometers (because temperatures typically drop noticeably and suddenly in the presence of paranormal activity) and two

A multitude of ghosts inhabit the Marshall House, a historic inn used as a Civil War hospital and morgue. A haunted room can be booked.

compasses (as spirit phenomena often have an electromagnetic effect). They were given all the rooms on the second floor with access to the entire hotel, from basement to roof. Half a dozen teams separated to investigate every corner of Marshall House.

A Searchers member named Paul had spent the day at Hodgson Hall, headquarters of the highly respected Georgia Historical Society. His research revealed that during Union occupation of Savannah, which began in December 1864 and continued until after the war's end in 1865, Marshall House had been used as a Union hospital. Many soldiers died and were buried beneath the building and adjacent Broughton Street.

Several guests have awakened to the feeling of a hand resting on their foreheads, as if a phantom Civil War physician were determining if they had a fever.

In the basement, Thomas registered a rapid drop in temperature and experienced physical pressure at her temples. Al Cobb and his family team heard a phantom cat scream loudly in the basement and son Jason witnessed a ghost cat walk through a wall. Father Cobb said hotel employees had observed the ghost of a Union officer, a little girl and a tabby cat.

Elsewhere in Marshall House, Searchers experienced cold spots, nausea, changes in air pressure, moving dark shadows and spinning compass needles. One team used an Ouija board and contacted a young girl who made a necklace of amethyst beads move. At a séance, a chandelier was set in motion. In a restroom, Thomas found three stalls with individual doors that extend from the floor to the ceiling. One was locked from within (more about that later).

At another séance in the basement, a pendulum was suspended, and spirits were requested to answer questions "with a vertical swing for yes and a horizontal swing for no," Thomas wrote. Making contact with a Union soldier, they asked for a physical sign. "This is really strange," said John. "I feel a wave of energy around my shoulders. It feels as if someone is tugging on my pants pocket." Another Searcher, Deb, said she felt someone softly running his fingers through her hair.

After finally crashing for the night, two roommates heard a metallic clicking sound outside their door for several hours.

The Searchers' photographs yielded a wealth of spheres, or "spirit balls," and gray shadows, and their audio tape revealed slamming doors, heavy footsteps followed by a dragging sound, scrapping and garbled talking—the usual paranormal fare.

The Automatic Typist and Locked Johnnie

Nancy Roberts tells a Marshall House story in *Ghosts from the Coast*. Sue and Richard Martin were down from fabled Gettysburg, Pennsylvania, to enjoy Savannah's most exciting celebration: St. Patrick's Day. They gambled on obtaining accommodations and made no reservations, arriving to find no rooms available in the city's many bed-and-breakfast inns. The Marshall House offered them its last room, and the offer was gratefully accepted. Mr. Martin was intrigued by the hotel's Civil War history. As the couple prepared to walk to the riverfront, they thought they heard the sound of an old-fashioned typewriter in the next room. Downstairs in the restroom, Mrs. Martin found all three stalls locked from the inside but apparently vacant. The reaction of the desk clerk to this news was, "Again?"

Room for One

Later that night, Sue fell asleep, but Richard was restless. He decided to go to the car for a book but became confused in the hotel's narrow hallways. Hearing footsteps descending the stairs, he stepped aside as a man appeared, holding the front of a stretcher. The stretcher arrived holding the form of a tall man covered with a white sheet, followed by a second apparent hospital attendant. The two bearers spoke in voices that seemed muffled. The dead patient was named Wright, and they were taking him to the morgue in the basement, which made both men uncomfortable.

Martin stood still, stunned by the tableau, and then realized the two men were returning with the now empty stretcher. One turned to him and pointed for him to get on it. Martin managed to croak out, "No," and the phantoms disappeared.

Naturally, Martin slept poorly that night. At breakfast, he asked a waiter about strange activity in the basement. The employee explained that he only worked days and had experienced nothing unusual, but the night staff spoke as if ghosts constantly paraded on the stairs and through the halls. The bones of a tall man had been found in the basement during renovation, he recalled. The waiter also explained that famed Georgia author Joel Chandler Harris, who had married a Savannah woman and wrote several of his stories there, had occupied the room adjacent to theirs. The self-locking restroom doors were supposedly a legacy of parties held for the wedding, when young women crowded the facilities.

In his book *Haunted Savannah*, James Caskey reported that workers restoring the Marshall House found rotted floorboards in a lower room. After removing the wood, they found skeletal remains—separate bundles of arms and legs and hands and feet. Caskey believed doctors gathered a day's worth of amputations and buried them under the floor, where they remained until 1999.

"There are some weird sounds down there," ventured a security guard. "Sounds that shouldn't be there."

Also downstairs is the night manager's office, where weird events started after the removal of the bones. Effects included footsteps and moans, and the shadowy figure of a one-armed Union soldier clad in a heavy, dark blue overcoat passing the office door. One manager reported papers would resequence themselves and switch piles, while money was restacked. That manager told the spirits that she understood good clean fun. "But please don't play with the money," she requested. The ghosts complied with this reasonable request.

Ghost Hounds has held their Ghostock meeting at the Marshall House. In December 2005, Denisee called the hotel about her reservation and asked after recent activity. The clerk instantly replied, "I was sitting at my desk when I heard a tick, tick, tick. I thought it was a clock, but there isn't a clock like that here around my desk. So, I turned around and the lock on one of the cabinets was swinging all by itself and making the tick, tick, tick sound. I told whomever it was to stop. I turned back around to my desk and the lock ticked three more times and then stopped." Occasionally, while sitting at her desk, the clerk would feel a cat rubbing against her leg and attempt to pet it before remembering it was a phantom animal.

After the January 2006 Ghostock, Denisee related on the Ghost Hounds website, "My dear hubby said that the first night, he felt like someone was pushing down on his legs while he was sleeping. It woke him up! He looked up and saw (there was enough light because I insisted there be a bit of light on while staying in the most haunted hotel in the world) that there was a tiny throw pillow on his leg, but it felt like something weighing at least forty pounds was on his legs." She concluded by stating, "We definitely heard sounds of people moving about but couldn't find where they were originating from." They also noted lighting issues.

Goohsmom said that on two nights there was a "very strong smell of cigarette smoke in our room" when no one was around, a smell stronger than when smokers were standing around and puffing away.

During a film screening, Hoot-n-Howl felt a phantom tap on the shoulder, a light, three finger female tap seeking her attention. Returning to her room, she found the do-not-disturb sign, which had been left hanging on the exterior door knob, on the inside knob, and the beds made. "As I walked by the bathroom, I got the intense feeling that someone was in the bathroom." She hurried out and confirmed that her roomie, Denise, had not touched the sign or made the beds, and she had felt a presence in the bathroom when they first arrived. Returning to the room, where they had left the thermostat at sixty-five, they found it reset to ninety. At the front desk, Hoot-n-Howl was told that in no circumstances did their employees violate the do-not-disturb signs. Then, she "said that just the other day a gentleman staying up there came down complaining that someone had removed the sign from his door and had come in and done some cleaning," and the temperature had been cranked up. Hoot-n-Howl concluded, "That clerk was pretty freaked out."

Hkolin wrote that her husband, Dave, was sitting at the desk in their room, placed right beside the door, when the handle started jiggling. Believing it was Hkolin, he immediately opened the door but saw no one anywhere in the hall.

Although no children were in the hotel that weekend, on Friday, Supergirl slept little "due to the sound of little feet running up and down the hall." Debilee and her husband detected the phantom smoke for several nights, and on two nights "heard lots of children running the halls" and raising quite a "ruckus."

Pingghosthunter and his wife heard the ghostly children's footsteps, plus loud rapping, coming from the outside wall on the second floor.

In Room 213, Darkness Waits was watching TV at 10:00 p.m. when she heard some unexpected sounds: "The water in my bathtub turned on by itself…I turned off the faucet and said out loud, 'Thank you…but I'm not ready yet to take my bath.'" The fixture then behaved itself.

Ghostgeek was taking a nap before a midnight trip to Bonaventure Cemetery when she was awakened by "the sound of someone walking loudly in high heels on the floor above me. Unmistakable 'clack, clack, clack' sound of a woman walking in heels on a bare, wood floor. I could tell they were walking from one side of the bed to the other, into the bathroom, out again, repeat over and over and over. Would stop for a few seconds, then start again—went on for a good ten minutes or more." Later, describing the event to other attendees, she said her room number was 205 and wondered who was in 305. "We were," responded Supergirl, explaining that she had brought no heels to the hotel and the room was unoccupied when the incident occurred.

Sunday night at 3:00 a.m., Cbreck and her roommate were startled by "a very loud crash in the hallway of the fourth floor," followed by several minutes of a cart traveling down the hall, and another loud crash. "Then strange tappings on our door! Then another round of the cart being pushed. We also heard what seemed to be a female voice talking. It sounded muffled and distant. All of this...and nobody was there!"

Eviljim was pleased upon his return to Room 418 on Friday to find robes and chocolates laid out and music issuing from the CD player. He cut off the music and left for dinner, returning to find the CD player operating again. When his wife, Jane, asked why the CD was playing, it stopped. The do-not-disturb sign, left outside, was found inside.

Y'ALL: The Magazine of Southern People dispatched Meredith Dabbs across the South for an article titled the "Haunted South." Dabbs heard that the Marshall House was haunted by soldiers, children and a cat. Her first night was quiet, but footsteps were heard passing and stopping at her door. On the second night, she wrote, "I heard a little bell ringing up and down the hall along with the heavy footsteps that stomped at my doorway." During the next night, a bag of candy left on a nightstand "mysteriously fell to the floor." The incidents left Dabbs "more than ready to pack up and head home" and recommended that the non–thrill seeker bring a nightlight. She wrote, "[I was] convinced that I encountered the soldier, the cat, and the children playing underneath my bed."

In June 2004, my wife, Earline, and I spent two nights in the Marshall House, hoping for a paranormal experience. Unfortunately, typing sounds were not heard from rooms, the women's bathroom stalls were unlocked (I sent Earline in) and no spectral stretcher bearers invited me to hop on for a one-way ride. There is apparently something wrong with my psychic aura, for over the past thirty years, I have spent more time on Civil War battlefields than anyone who doesn't work for the National Park Service, taken thousands of photographs and encountered nothing but bugs and annoying tourists. Perhaps I should be thankful.

Savannah's City of the Dead

One scary story was related by Al Cobb in his book *Savannah's Ghosts*, a follow-up to his creepy debut, *Danny's Bed: A Tale of Savannah Poltergeists*, which

The Confederate section at Savannah's Laurel Grove Cemetery. This spooky figure watches over the honored dead.

is a disturbing and exciting read. A group of Searchers was given a nighttime lantern tour of Laurel Grove Cemetery, one of Savannah's oldest and most historic burying grounds. It was a quiet night and the members learned a lot of local history through the lives of those buried in Laurel Grove, but then they entered the Confederate plot known as the Gettysburg Section.

In the early 1870s, Confederate graves on the battlefield at Gettysburg, Pennsylvania, were opened and the remains sent to Georgia, Virginia, North Carolina and South Carolina. The bones of 101 Southern soldiers were buried there; the other 600 Confederates in this section died on garrison duty or defending Savannah, including the action at Fort McAllister.

Psychic and Searchers member Bobbie Weyl was immediately overwhelmed by the number of spirits that demanded her attention and caused a tremendous feeling of sadness. She saw in her mind an officer named James John. Beside him was a seventeen-year-old infantryman whose voice sounded as if it originated from a deep well. Through his eyes, she witnessed the boy's final moments in hand-to-hand combat, scenes like reenactments shown on documentaries. At the end, she saw a bayonet penetrate his chest and heard the boy's wild scream of pain. He slowly bled to death.

Weyl was visibly upset by the experience and felt her strength evaporate. She grew dizzy, and her legs gave way. As Kathy Thomas led her away, the young Confederate implored, "Lady, come back! Please, come back!"

At home, still shaken, Weyl prepared a snack before bed. She was surprised to find herself singing "Annabel Lee," a Civil War song she had never heard before. Apparently, the Confederate spirits in Laurel Grove Cemetery had implanted the song in her mind.

Al Cobb and his son Jason had been walking through the cemetery when Jason pointed out a row of graves ahead and predicted that a Cobb was buried there. Al's flashlight revealed a stone that read "J.A. Cobb," which are his son's initials.

Civil War Antics in Colonial Cemetery

Savannah's oldest burial ground is Colonial Cemetery, where the original colonists are buried. While not ghostly, we must report some ghoulish activities practiced by Union soldiers during the winter of 1864–65. Remains were robbed of valuables, and vaults were emptied of human remains to provide shelter from winter weather. Bored soldiers also screwed with the engravings. We find that Captain Jonathan Cooper died at the age of 1700, while Phillip D. Woolhopter was only 1491. Joseph Muir, who died at 11, left a 17-year-old wife, Mary, and a son, Lewis, 12. Susannah Gray died July 26, 1812, at 121 years, 1124 days.

Bummer

In *Ghosts from the Coast*, Nancy Roberts related the tale of Glenn and Iris Cranston, Atlantans who honeymooned in Savannah. They were drawn to dine at the Moon River Brewery Company (21 West Bay Street) because of the famous song by native wordsmith Johnny Mercer. The owner gave them a tour of the historic structure (1819), designed by renowned architect William Jay.

After ordering, Iris realized she had left her bag upstairs and went to retrieve it. The owner stopped by the table to share the story of the resident ghost, a Civil War bummer who was a Union renegade that broke into the building and was killed by the inhabitants. The staff had heard disembodied voices, footsteps and the sound of something being dragged across the floor, presumably the family secretly disposing of a Federal soldier during Savannah's occupation. The ghostly activity occurred, of course, on the second floor. When the building was renovated the skeleton of a man, judged to date from the Civil War, was found sealed in a basement well.

Iris soon returned, shaken, telling of a tall man who had blocked her return and then reached for her before disappearing—undoubtedly the slain yet still unrepentant bummer.

In July 2002, the Searchers arranged for a ghost hunt at Moon River. Among the six members was author Al Cobb, who described the experience in *Savannah's Ghosts II*. One waitress, Ryan Dill, has heard her name called when she was alone, and many strange sounds have been heard in the basement. Fellow worker Erica Taylor has a strong feeling of constant surveillance. She has unpleasant feelings in the basement and downstairs rooms and was once touched by a hand that was not there. On occasion, table candles on the first floor spontaneously ignite. According to Cobb, each member of the Seekers team "felt at least some of the psychic vibrations reported by the waitresses."

The Moon River Brewing Company was constructed in 1821 by Charlestonian Elazer Early as the City Hotel and also housed branches of the U.S. Post Office and the Bank of the United States. Revolutionary War hero Marquis de Lafayette, Mexican War general Winfield Scott and naturalist James Audubon, who lived there for six months while seeking a publisher for his wildlife sketches, were guests. Pete Wittberger improved the establishment in 1851, adding live male and female lions, and the hotel closed operations shortly before Sherman occupied the town. In later years, it was used as a warehouse and office supply store. It became Moon River in 1999.

Historic Ghost Watch settled teams into the pub on May 27, 2006, from 1:00 to 3:00 a.m., with six members split into two teams and a base unit. In the downstairs dining area, investigators felt sad, ill and weak, and one psychic saw a blond man with a mustache sadly hammering a wall with one hand. They also heard a "foot scrapping."

The poolroom and bar provided a heavy presence and a psychic sighting of a shadow showing a head and shoulders. Breathing was heard from behind the bar. Foot dragging was heard by the base team at the entrance and in the dining room all three team members heard foot scraping that came when they were asking questions seeking EVPs in a third floor room. On the second floor, footsteps were heard descending the stairs. The second floor also evidenced a growl, an abrupt temperature drop of fifteen degrees and a feeling of being threatened. A cold spot was followed around the second floor. As a team ascended stairs to the fourth floor, one member felt a pain in his leg, stating, "[His] entire left leg is in severe pain," which ceased when he returned to the third floor. EVPs included "I died over here," "Tell me," "Talk to me longer," a moan, a whisper and four intermingled voices. The report stated that a cold spot "appeared to follow a team for several minutes across two floors."

During a Ghoststock meeting in Savannah in 2005, members of Ghost Hounds investigated Moon River. In a back room Babs "felt as if [she] passed by someone," detected a heaviness, saw a shadow and heard an unexplainable sound. While photographing the haunted stairs, she made a few observations: "I noticed a man standing next to me arching his neck forward to see what I was taking a picture of." But no one was there. During a party at Moon River, Christina, a friend of Jamie Caskey, was in the basement when she "had a brush with some sort of presence" that left her "shaking, pale and covered in goosebumps."

In 2007, the *South* magazine was doing a photo shoot at Moon River. Participants "heard footsteps and strange noises," according to Katrina Sage. The crew was "just standing around discussing ideas when the strobes on the lights just kept going off." At first, they thought it was a problem with an automatic function, then realized that it was turned off.

As they were shooting, a large scrim "came crashing down." Sage recalled, "I was ready to call it a wrap. Whatever roams the halls on this floor was ready for us to head home." Investigators for a TAPS television episode captured on film a short humanoid creature running behind pool tables in the basement.

Moonlight and the Magnolia Inn

Guerard Hayward prospered in the cotton exporting business and used some of his fortune to construct his Savannah mansion in 1878. Unfortunately, his luck soon turned. In 1884, Hayward died after consuming bad seafood, and the boll weevil destroyed the South's cotton, leaving his wife, Pauline, and their children penniless. Pauline became a midwife, delivering many of Savannah's citizens in her home.

In 1984, the steamboat Gothic structure was transformed into the Magnolia Place Inn, a bed-and-breakfast, where patrons and staff have both experienced the supernatural. An author conducting Civil War research in Savannah announced at breakfast one morning that he had awakened during the night to find a soldier, clad in a ragged dirty uniform, standing beside his bed.

Alan Brown, author of *Stories from the Haunted South*, and his wife, Marilyn, spent a memorable night at the inn. During the early morning hours of July 24, 2002, Marilyn awoke her husband with a bizarre story. Awakened by a call of nature, she suddenly heard "a loud buzzing in the room," like electricity. The noise moved and made half the hair on her head stand on end. She attempted to rouse Alan, but found herself paralyzed, stating, "I felt something heavy was keeping me from moving...I was scared to death."

Other guests have felt cold spots and an unseen presence downstairs, and employees have encountered wet footprints and a Victorian-era gentleman sipping brandy and smoking a cigar—he disappeared, but the smoke lingered.

Girl Scouts from around the world make pilgrimages to Savannah to visit founder Juliette Gordon Low's birthplace on East Oglethorpe Avenue. The house, constructed in 1820, may be haunted by her parents, once divided by death, now and forever more united in death. William W. Gordon died first, leaving his widow, Nellie, in deep mourning. When Nellie died, Margaret Gordon, a daughter-in-law, and the longtime family butler saw William walking out of the room, apparently returned to lead his beloved wife to paradise. They had first been separated by the Civil War, when William served with the Georgia Hussars and Nellie's brothers fought for the Union—one was killed, the other captured in combat.

PART III
CONFEDERATE GHOSTS OF CENTRAL GEORGIA

Central Georgia was the engine of the Confederacy, providing many troops for the military while civilian workers grew food in the fields, produced military goods in factories and cared for thousands of casualties in hospitals. Civil War–related spooks still reside in the cities and countryside.

MACON

The Spirit in the Chapel

Mercer University's Willingham Chapel seems to harbor several ghosts. Policeman John Morgan was inspecting the building at 2:00 a.m. one night when he heard footsteps from the empty balcony. However, those footsteps were on wood, and the balcony floor is concrete. The spirits were out this night, for continuing his rounds in the basement auditorium, he encountered a column of freezing air. The surrounding air was warm, but that one spot was frigid. Drama students of the Back Door Theater believe a ghost they call Oscar moves props, manipulates the lighting and once nearly struck a student with a plank. Another security guard has witnessed a woman in a long black dress. During the early 1900s, many students believed a Confederate officer or soldier who was killed there during the Civil War haunted Willingham. Several students witnessed the ghost.

A Salute from Fallen Comrades

The Columns, formerly Beall's 1850 Restaurant (315 College Street), was constructed just in time to perhaps capture a Civil War ghost or two. Originally Georgian, the building was transformed to a spectacular Greek Revival in 1901. The grand structure fell into disrepair but blossomed as a popular restaurant.

Barbara Duffey, Eatonton's celebrated author, reported in *Banshees, Bugles, and Belles* that in 1994, a group of reenactors of the Twelfth Georgia Regiment had a full-dress dinner in the upstairs banquet hall of Beall's. As they ate, the lights on two huge antique brass chandeliers blinked off and on sequentially, one after another, "until they were all flickering at various intervals." That effect would have been impossible to produce by hand because both chandeliers were controlled by a single switch that turned all the lights on or off at once. The audience watched with fascinated awe and proposed that a true veteran of the Twelfth Georgia, composed largely of Macon residents, was saluting those who proudly carried on the name of his unit. Perhaps his spirit had returned and wished to make contact with new comrades.

In *Ghost Stories of Georgia*, Chris Wangler found that the Beall House was constructed by Nathan Beall, owner of several plantations. His son, George, joined the Forty-seventh Georgia in March 1863 and left to fight for the Confederacy. His regular letters home ceased a year later, but the family never learned his fate.

In 1860, daughter Juliet married a surgeon, George C. Griffin, who served with the Army of Northern Virginia. Reassigned to Macon in September 1863, he began his journey home but never completed it— he also disappeared. Juliet spent considerable time in her second-floor bedroom, watching the street below for George's return. With the death of his wife, Nathan sold the home to Leonidas A. Jordan and moved in with his daughter.

The 1842 Inn

John Greshan, mayor, attorney, judge and cotton merchant constructed the magnificent 1842 Inn, which has eighteen columns. Inn employee Joanne Dillard has never seen a ghost but does not discredit stories related by guests. One woman who had stayed in the Dogwood Room had been anxious because it had an outside entrance. After she showered and toweled off, she turned to find a man standing in her bedroom. Clad in a uniform with a long, dark jacket, the man smiled and bowed his head, as if to say, "Don't be afraid. I am here to protect you," Dillard related to Shelia Turnage in *Haunted Inns of the Southeast*. The guest felt "a warm, relaxed feeling" in her neck. After relating her story to the staff in the morning, a photograph of Greshan was proffered. The clothing was identical, and the woman believed it was a younger image of her ghostly but gallant intruder.

Ancient City of the Dead and Civil War Battlefield

In east Macon at Ocmulgee is an ancient mound city built by Native Americans. In November 1864, as Sherman headed to Milledgeville, he feinted on Macon, resulting in a skirmish on park grounds. Confederate fortifications are present in the park today. According to Master Ranger Sylvia Flowers, who had worked at Ocmulgee for twenty years, she received "very sincere" calls from visitors who reported a Confederate soldier with cape strolling across the grounds. "That's logical since a battle was fought here, and surely people were killed," she stated.

Flowers said that on her way to her first day of work at Ocmulgee, she stopped at a convenience store, where someone told her, "You know, that place is haunted."

For decades, residents of Summit Avenue have reported the ghost of a headless Confederate soldier haunting the grounds of the McLeon-Melrose-Barton House. Unlike most decapitated spirits, this one occasionally has his head in hand, literally.

Elak Swindell led his EOPS group on a ghost-hunting expedition to Macon on August 15–20, 2003. At Rose Hill Cemetery they recorded sixty-six "clear and interesting EVPs," including male voices saying, "Pass within, but you will help out," "How was it?" and "It was tight." To Swindell, this suggested that a Civil War prison camp occupied the site, and "a large quantity of the EVPs concerned prisoners and wartime situations."

Follow the Bouncing Cannonball: Ghosts of the Cannonball House

Two brief attacks against Macon produced only one act of destruction. During a July raid, a single cannonball hit the sidewalk in front of Judge

The Cannonball House in Macon suffered the city's only damage during the war. The presences of wartime occupants are still felt.

Asa Holt's house, pierced a column and bounced into the parlor. The Cannonball House, an elegant 1853 Greek Revival structure, has been restored to a Civil War setting. In the old servant's quarters behind the house is a Confederate museum.

EOPS concluded that the Cannonball House was haunted by seven to eight ghosts, particularly an old woman who died in the gift shop area when it was an apartment, and an angry man who killed himself with a shotgun. This ghost EVPed, "Don't ever come back," and another male EVP said, "Young bidding for the fire," accompanied by the sound of a stamp banging onto an ink pad and papers. Swindell proposed that the house was used as a recruiting station for signing up men for the war. "Other war-related vocal exchanges were also recorded," Swindell reported.

One of the female ghosts was seen by two visitors in recent years as she admired herself in a mirror: "She was fully visible from the waist up, but her legs were invisible." One of the ghosts, or maybe it was a team competition, occasionally relocated a cannonball kept to represent the Civil War attack.

Another Dead Yankee Tale

Macon's Gaugh House (172 Cleveland Avenue), a one-story, Greek Revival structure, was built in 1836 for D.D. Sanders. There is a story that during the Civil War, a Union soldier stationed at a nearby camp was drunk and disorderly on the street. Fearing for the safety of his children, a caretaker attempted to chase the soldier off. The Yankee resisted and died in the resulting struggle. Fearing the repercussions that would certainly fall on the man and owners of the property, the soldier was quietly buried on the grounds. For many years, children in the Vineville area feared the soldier's ghost that was said to haunt the area.

WARNER ROBINS

Everyone Must Get a Stone

On their initial date, Christine S. Camp and Ashley Cox visited his parent's home in Warner Robins, a relatively new community established for a military base during World War II. They were in a sitting room as darkness fell, and when Christine walked down a dim hall toward the kitchen, she "saw a large-boned man in a gray uniform with a large brass belt buckle on it," she wrote in *FATE* magazine.

Ashley denied having Confederate ancestors, although he had a passionate interest in the Civil War, had amassed a large collection of books on the subject and collected military artifacts. Christine was certain that a family member of his had fought for the Confederacy, for each time she visited her parents-in-law, "the gray-uniformed man appeared; it was as if he were trying to tell me something."

After their marriage, Christine and Ashley went through his family albums and discovered John Augustus Cox, Ashley's great-grandfather, who had indeed participated in the War Between the States. Christine addressed her ghost as "Johnny," and the spirit adopted the couple, moving to various residences with them.

The ancestral Cox home was in Plains, so the couple began their research there. They interviewed Alton Carter, a brother of President Jimmy Carter's father. When Alton had initially arrived in Plains, he lived with Johnny (called Gus) and his wife, Sarah. Alton recalled Johnny speaking of his war experiences in the Confederate cavalry.

When Christine and Ashley lived on St. Simons Island, Johnny repeatedly showed himself to two of their friends, who saw "a very sad and puzzled look on his face." Christine resolved to help Johnny find peace.

The couple traveled to the state archives in Atlanta and found three men named John A. Cox, but they could not identify any of them as Ashley's great-grandfather. That night, Christine experienced a dream in which she saw a gravestone bearing the name of John A. Cox and an indistinguishable battalion number leaning against a rural garage. In the morning, she described the site to Ashley, who immediately recognized it as his Uncle Jack's house in Americus.

Unfortunately, Jack, the grandson of Johnny, was a loner and refused to interact with the family. The couple called Jack, but he refused to speak with them. Christine and Ashley drove to Americus when they knew Jack was absent and found the stone, which Jack had unaccountably kept for many years.

With the information on the stone, they identified Johnny and ordered a regulation military gravestone. The living and dead alike awaited its delivery with anticipation, as Johnny appeared much more frequently than normal. When Christine photographed Ashley, dressed in a Confederate uniform, beside the marker, she spied Johnny watching from a window of their home, "a smile on his face."

The pair drove to the Plains of Lebanon Cemetery in Sumter County, dragged the stone to Johnny's grave, dug a hole and placed the monument, eighty years tardy. They also left a Confederate flag on the plot.

Johnny found peace and has not appeared since, although Christine sometimes feels his presence. Ashley has joined the Sons of Confederate Veterans, portrays a Southern soldier at reenactments and writes Civil War articles. Christine is proud because, despite her Northern origins, she was instrumental in helping her husband and Johnny find "their place."

FORSYTH

School Spirits

We now enter an unnatural situation: ghosts of the dead in a dead college. I have often teased my wife, Earline, a proud "polished cornerstone" of Tift College, about her deceased alma mater. The school started life in 1849 as the Forsyth Collegiate Institute. Only fifteen years later, war reached Georgia, and thousands of Confederate casualties flowed down the railroad to dozens of towns, Forsyth among them. In 1864, hundreds of wounded and sick soldiers flooded the railroad depot in Forsyth from battlefields around Atlanta. A wooded grove separated the tracks from the school, and the college president, Dr. W.C. Walker, had eight hundred tents, each with wooden floors and properly trenched for drainage, set up in that area. Bowers of tree limbs were constructed, and cots were lined with leaves. The college building itself housed the medical center and the most seriously afflicted men. Operations were performed beneath the trees.

Nearly every able-bodied citizen of Forsyth responded to the crises. People bearing food and fresh water met the trains. Soldiers were transported in private carriages and wagons, fine linen and bed clothing were ripped up for bandages and all manner of supplies were donated. Women of the community, particularly students of the school, nursed 1,800 suffering men under the supervision of local doctors. Walker's wife, an herbalist, brought her natural remedies for the relief of the wounded.

Hundreds of soldiers died of wounds, infection, pneumonia and typhoid. Rest Haven Cemetery has a special section containing 299 unknown Confederates, one identified soldier and one known nurse, Honora Sweney.

When the Civil War ended, the school was in ruins, but President Walker, college trustees and churches across the state rallied to restore the educational institution. It was renamed Monroe Female College and then Bessie Tift College for the wife of a generous benefactor. The building that housed the hospital was destroyed by fire in 1879, and it was replaced by the present Ponder Hall several years later.

Ghosts from the Civil War years concentrated their attention on Tift Dorm, which stood from 1901 until 1972. The primary specter may have been Honora's spirit, but campus lore maintained that it was a young woman named Bessie, although not the school's namesake. For many years, Bessie roamed Tift Dorm late at night. Hundreds of students heard her heels tapping down the halls as she made her rounds, stopping to test every doorknob. Brave young ladies who waited and snatched open their doors at the spook's approach saw nothing. But after they closed the door, the ghost was heard continuing down the hall.

The popular, romantic legend was that Bessie was a student in the 1860s that cared for the casualties. She fell in love with one lad, but he succumbed to his wounds. Bessie then contracted typhoid fever. Knowing her demise was imminent Bessie—or Honora, as some insist—requested that she be buried among the soldiers in the cemetery. Ever since, she has trod the halls of the school searching for her soldier lover. She is one of the only women in the state interred amid Confederate soldiers. A Georgia historical marker at the cemetery honors her service.

Tift Dorm also contained two male ghosts. One opened the door to room fifty-nine every night. Two roommates, Sandra Burnett and Gail Davidson, reported that at 7:10 each morning, they heard a man with a crippled leg make his way down the hall. They always heard step, drag, step, drag. In November 1971, they were asleep when Sandra felt her bed being pushed. In the darkened room she asked Gail if she was moving about. Gail was not, and as she looked over at Sandra's bed she distinguished a black shape standing over her roomie. Other doors in Tift Dorm opened by themselves, footsteps and heavy breathing were heard outside room doors and, in the bathrooms, water faucets turned on and off without cause.

Just before Tift Dorm was demolished, someone snapped a photo of it. When developed, it seemed to show the ghostly faces of two young men,

Although older haunted buildings were demolished, Tift College's ghosts transferred their residences to newer structures.

sixteen or seventeen years old, peering out different windows. Presumably they were young soldiers who died somewhere on the grounds of the school. A huge print displayed in Lies Hall was carefully scrutinized by countless students and rarely failed to produce shudders.

Students also detected at least one male ghost, dubbed Jefferson, who died at the Civil War hospital and haunted Lies Dorm, searching for the peace he never found in this life. A ghost in West Dorm also opened the door to one particular room each evening. (A ghostly incident involving my wife and me is related in another book about Georgia's college ghosts.)

It is good to know that Tift College's ghosts were capable of vacating one structure and transporting their essence to newer ones. After all, it is probably the land that is haunted, not the buildings. Tift College may be gone, but its school spirits live on.

The Ghost Dog of the Civil War

Across the street from Tift College are three remarkably preserved railroad structures. The Victorian Old Train Depot (1898) was restored in 1993 and hosts a local history museum. Beside it is the restored freight depot (1917), but the most important is the original railroad depot, a stone structure from 1846, where many trains arrived with wounded and sick Confederates from the extended fighting around Atlanta in 1864.

In 2002, W.J. "Buddy" Mitchell wrote the "Ghost Dog of Forsyth, Georgia," a version told around town since 1865, and posted it on the historical society's website.

In the fall of 1863, a county resident named Aaron turned eighteen and elected to join his older brother fighting Northern aggression in Virginia. Aaron's faithful dog, Sam, followed the young man everywhere, so before he left, Aaron tied Sam to a tree with a leather plow line. Aaron had walked half the distance to Forsyth when Sam appeared beside him. Aaron continued into town and encountered his friend Fred, transferring mail from the depot to the post office. Fred volunteered to return Sam home the following day, and Aaron departed for the front. Fred fulfilled his promise, but on his return to town, Sam caught up with him. Fred decided to adopt Sam for the duration, and the dog soon started greeting every hospital train that arrived at the depot and, without fail, visited each hospital daily. When medical workers complained about the pooch's presence, the chief surgeon ordered that the dog be left alone "because

Sam was doing more good for the men than they could ever do" by reminding the patients of home. The wounded eagerly anticipated Sam's daily visit.

With the war over, Aaron returned home, and from his railroad car spotted Sam on the station's dock. As he left the train, Aaron looked anxiously for Sam, who had disappeared. When Fred arrived for the mail, Aaron said, "Where did Sam go? I thought I saw him."

"That's impossible," Fred replied sadly. He explained that several weeks earlier, Union cavalry had descended on Forsyth. Seeing Sam running past the invaders, a Union trooper asked locals what the story was. Told that Sam knew a train was approaching, the Federals rushed to capture the train, heedlessly trampling the canine to death. At the depot, the Federals were informed that the war had ended. Faithful Sam was picked up by a resident and lovingly buried beside the depot, where his spirit met his master returning from war.

BARNESVILLE

Not Gone with the Wind

Fred Crane, who played Brent Tarleton (one of Scarlet O'Hara's suitors in *Gone with the Wind*), and wife Terry retired from Hollywood and opened a bed-and-breakfast called Tarleton Oaks (Red Hill Inn, 643 Greenwood Street, 1859) in 2000. During the war, the house saw service as a Confederate headquarters and hospital. Locals witnessed a ghost attired in a gray uniform, rocking chairs move on their own for up to ten minutes, paintings rearrange themselves on the wall and fireplace screens that unaccountably fell over.

On February 21, 2005, in cooperation with the Atlanta FOX television channel, Historic Ghost Watch of Kennesaw explored Tarleton Oaks. Constructed in 1849 by Josiah Holmes, it was owned during the war by Charles Lambdin, who established Barnesville's first newspaper, and Gordon Military Institute. Near the war's end, two trains collided, killing 150 soldiers and sending many injured men to houses along the railroad, including Tarleton Oaks. Owners and guests have glimpsed a Confederate soldier and a woman dressed in black and heard three children playing in the attic. Historic Ghost Watch deployed two teams composed of six members and a base with two.

In Rhett's Suite, Team One "surprised something," as one member "saw something move quickly from the couch." A presence was felt and two cameras flashed spontaneously. In Scarlett's Suite, all members, including the FOX cameraman, found a "significantly hotter area in the middle of the room," and a presence was detected and followed by one member until the spirit became upset.

Team Two had a camera die in the library, and a second flashed twice on its own. In Rhett's Suite, one camera malfunctioned, and the flash on another started going off by itself. The dining room produced a "masculine 'woodsy' smell" and a feeling of discomfort. Two members sat at a table and asked questions for EVP reply. One question was answered by two distinct knocks. In Ashley's Suite, a woman was overcome by "an overwhelming feeling of sadness," which dissipated when she changed location. A camera at the site "flashed rapidly six or seven times." The woman said, "If you want Ed to stop taking pictures in here, make his camera flash once." The camera complied and then flashed twice more. In Melanie's Suite, a female presence was felt.

The Base Team "heard whispering and giggling on the porch" like "girls whispering to each other." Fifteen minutes later, one man heard "a female voice behind him say his name."

Many electromagnetic anomalies and EVPs were recorded in a number of locations in the mansion. Historic Ghost Watch found "a great deal of activity" at Tarleton Oaks and considered it as "quite possibly, one of the most haunted homes [they had] investigated."

Crane closed Tarleton Oaks to shelter relatives left destitute by Hurricane Katrina in New Orleans, and it never reopened. In March 2007, he sold his extensive collection of GWTW memorabilia. Crane died in August 2008, at age ninety. He had spoken the first lines in the movie: "What do we care if we were expelled from college, Scarlett? The war is going to start any day now, so we'd have left college anyhow." To this Scarlett replied, "Fiddle-dee-dee. War, war, war. This war talk's spoiling all the fun at every party this spring. I get so bored I could scream." His twin was played by George Reeves, who became television's Superman.

Grantville

In 1897, J.W. Colley and his wife, Itura, constructed Bonnie Castle (2 Post Street), a twenty-room, five-thousand-square-foot Romanesque Revival Victorian home in Grantville. The brick house, with Stone Mountain granite, has heart pine flooring. The family was involved in textiles, land, agriculture and banking, with interests in politics and art. In recent history, the house was converted into a bed-and-breakfast.

The Civil War Room in the inn was equipped with two beds used in a Civil War hospital established at Fort McAllister, perhaps the bombproof that produced paranormal images on photographic film described earlier. Terry Kimbrell of the Foundation for Paranormal Research photographed the room during an investigation of the inn and one picture revealed a mist hovering above the floor and a white blob at the ceiling.

Along Comes Mary

Bonnie Castle became a favorite place for foundation members, who regularly visited in teams and always encountered some strange activity. Orbs were common—even to the naked eye—nine EVPs were recorded and a ghost cat was spotted. The orbs seemed to originate in the attic, where the Civil War room was located, and dispersed to second floor rooms.

Over the years, many groups of ghost hunters paraded through the establishment, capturing many orbs on still and video cameras. The orbs were all sizes, varied widely in intensity and moved in every direction. Some were so predictable in their behavior that they were recognized as individual creations.

Bonnie Castle, a National Register property, has also closed.

Newnan

Christina A. Barber is a novelist who caught the ghost-hunting bug while researching a book. She has since written a ghost book titled *Spirits of Georgia's Southern Crescent*, concentrating on Newnan, her home, and west central Georgia.

The Soldier Boy in the Girl's School

College Temple Girls School operated on College Street in Newnan from 1853 to 1889. Although classes continued during the war, the facility was utilized as a Confederate hospital. Later, most of the buildings were demolished, but two survived as homes.

A realtor (who knows better than anyone the community's ghosts) told Barber that he first sold one of the buildings a number of years earlier. The owner told him that a ghostly figure haunted a particular hall, pacing up and down and dragging his boots. "But he's very friendly as long as you whistle 'Dixie,'" the man was assured. The realtor laughed, thinking his leg was being pulled, but the lady was insistent. "If you hear or see anything strange, just whistle Dixie and it will be alright," she insisted. Later asked to resell the home, the realtor asked the recent owner if anything strange had happened in the house. "Of course," she replied, "we'd just whistle 'Dixie' and everything was fine."

When the house was sold again, the realtor met a colleague for a walk through the property. As they reached the third floor, every door on that level suddenly opened in unison. One presumes the visitors then whistled in unison.

Another Newnan Civil War ghost story related by Barber comes from a parking lot on Madison Street that provides access to the back entries of businesses on Jefferson Street. One night, a waitress who left a restaurant shortly returned with a shocking story to tell. She was about to enter her car when she heard someone beside her. Turning, she found a tall man in unusual clothing and hat who asked her destination before vanishing. Others who have encountered this rare talking spirit testify that it was wearing a Confederate uniform.

The Ghost at Powers Crossroads

The Powers Mansion, an elegant, three-story structure located at Powers Crossroads on the Franklin Highway, is located ten miles west of Newnan in Coweta County. It has remained in the hands of the original family since its construction in the early 1800s. On October 28, 1979, the *Atlanta Journal Constitution Sunday Magazine* wrote "Old Haunts," describing Tom Powers, who, for forty years, was a resident who knew of extensive psychic phenomena on the property. Powers—a writer, painter and psychic—founded the long-running Powers Crossroads Country Fair in 1971.

"Oh, yes, there are ghosts," Powers said. "And there are poltergeists—mischievous little devils. There are five ghosts, and they're all quite friendly. They date back to the Civil War. We've had many séances here. The spiritual concentration at the house is quite powerful, really very remarkable."

The mansion's myriad ghosts included three seen frequently, and "all had tragic or sudden deaths—they got caught in the bind between life and death unexpectedly and must linger here because of that."

One of them was a Union officer caught pillaging the house in the summer of 1864, just after the battle of Atlanta was fought. Powers's great-great-grandmother took care of the situation: "[She] shot him, and he managed to crawl upstairs to the third story and died there. We see him now, in his uniform, in a sort of vapor. His spirit is very definitely there. I'm not the only one who has seen him."

Powers also tells the story of his great-aunt Mattie, who "died very suddenly of malaria one summer. It was a horrible shock. She had a little yellow cat, and the cat pined so badly for her that it died about four days later. We see them now, together, walking on the grounds."

The scariest ghost on the property is that of a sharecropper's wife, whose husband discovered her having an affair with another tenant farmer. The husband "killed her by cutting her head off. Occasionally, someone sees her walking the highways at night, carrying her head in her hands."

Since childhood, Powers knew that the land was haunted and "[had] a life of its own." Some people in the community practiced voodoo as well, according to Powers: "I'd hear their drums late at night. The place is very definitely haunted."

The Phantom Attack

Todd was an airman stationed at Aviano Air Base in Italy. On a visit home to Newnan, he and a friend decided to chase ghosts at Bethel Church in Senoia. Todd believed fighting occurred there during the Civil War, and others had reported paranormal activity. The pair circled the church on foot several times, hearing "the sounds of wolves and coyotes," which "were getting closer and much louder." Todd's companion fell into a trance and led him toward a grave. By this time, Todd was concerned—the air temperature had "dropped significantly," he "heard loud footsteps that seemed to be right next to [him]" and he "was hearing someone yell a battle cry."

The friend pointed out a particular grave and fainted. Todd shone his flash on the grave but the light abruptly ceased functioning. As more phantom footsteps approached, Todd revived his buddy, and they fled for his truck. Todd attempted to start the engine, but it refused to crank. Looking nervously toward the woods, he saw what appeared to be fog rolling in. "And fog does not move that fast," he stated. The engine finally caught, and the men hurried home to Newnan.

ANDERSONVILLE IN COWETA COUNTY

In March 1996, TNT premiered Andersonville, a two-part miniseries directed by the legendary John Frankenheimer. The filming had started two years earlier and 125 miles distant from the original prison camp—a full-scale replica was constructed on a dairy farm near Senoia in Coweta County. Hundreds of primitive dwellings, called shebangs, were constructed and three thousand extras hired for background scenes. These included actors, reenactors, college students, homeless people and off-duty soldiers as well as two hundred flat people—human-shaped plywood cutouts with photographs of people laminated onto them.

Thomas Porter, a screenwriter, signed on as one of the villains—a Raider—and described the experiences in the March–April 1996 issue of *Georgia Journal*. Early on, he wrote, a number of reenactors "claimed to have felt a strong physical presence on the set and in their camp."

One reenactor was Steve Enzweiler, a retired air force pilot and a professional artist and photographer. Enzweiler shot many rolls of film at the reenactment camp. One night, he photographed two men who stood in front of a tent, an empty chair separating them. When the film was developed and prints made, that shot showed "the faint outline of a third figure" sitting in the "empty" chair. "Visible is a bearded man looking into the camera, dressed in what appears to be a Union uniform," Porter wrote. Enzweiler examined the negative closely and pronounced it genuine.

THE DANGLING SPECTER OF WARM SPRINGS

In *Georgia's Ghostly Getaways*, Kathleen Walls wrote of a large, two-story antebellum house in Warm Springs, once the refuge and also the death site of President Franklin D. Roosevelt. It was owned by a wealthy man who left to fight for the Confederacy. His wife managed his affairs even as Atlanta was torched and Federals occupied their home. Informed that her husband had been killed, the woman either hanged herself or threw herself from the second floor. At the right angle and time of day, the shadow of the lady can be seen on a wall, leaping or hanging, according to your interpretation. "I have seen a shadow of a person on the wall of this house many times," said resident Johnny Craven.

LAGRANGE

"Lorena," a popular Civil War soldier's song, was written by H.D.L. Webster:

The years creep slowly by, Lorena,
The snow is on the grass again.
The sun's low down the sky, Lorena,
The frost gleams where the flow'rs have been.
But the heart throbs on as warmly now,
As when the summer days were nigh.
Oh, the sun can never dip so low
A-down affection's cloudless sky.

A hundred months have passed, Lorena,
Since last I held that hand in mine,
And felt the pulse beat fast, Lorena,
Though mine beat faster far than thine.
A hundred months, 'twas flowery May,
When up the hilly slope we climbed,
To watch the dying of the day,
And hear the distant church bells chime.

We loved each other then, Lorena,
More than we ever dared to tell,
And what we might have been, Lorena
Had but our loving prospered well—
But then, 'tis past, the years are gone,
I'll not call up their shadowy forms;
I'll say to them, 'Lost years, sleep on!
Sleep on! nor heed life's pelting storm.'

In *Georgia Ghosts*, Nancy Roberts tells of a Lieutenant John Griffin, who rode with Confederate general Joseph Wheeler's cavalry. As Sherman stalled before Atlanta, he dispatched his troopers to cut the railroads to Macon and Alabama and destroy Confederate supply trains and rail facilities. Union general Alexander McCook was to liberate the forty thousand Federals being held at Andersonville. A successful raid would wreak havoc behind enemy lines.

Vigilant Southern cavalry thwarted every Union maneuver, sorely embarrassing the Federal horsemen. McCook was turned back in fighting around Newnan, a hospital center, in an affair called the battle of Brown's Mill. There, Lieutenant Griffin was badly wounded in the right shoulder. After seeing all the Confederate wounded off to nearby Newnan, Griffin himself rode thirty-five miles to LaGrange, where his sister Indiana was attending LaGrange College. The buildings of the school also doubled as a military hospital.

Somehow Griffin avoided bleeding to death on the long journey and underwent surgery to remove the bullet. He awoke in Smith Hall, staring into the face of a beautiful girl known to history only as Lorena. She visited every day, tenderly washing his fever-flushed face. Of course, he fell in love with this ministering angel.

After a few days, Griffin's condition improved enough for him to join the convalescents at the grand Greek Revival mansion Bellevue, where he was placed in the large ballroom. Lorena visited faithfully, but Griffin's wound refused to heal and infection returned. With his mind affected by high fever, he would forget that his sweetheart had visited during the day. At night, Griffin stumbled out of bed and roamed the halls, grasping the arms of young nurses and crying, "Lorena!" Griffin died, deliriously calling for his lover.

Lieutenant Griffin's ghost, clad in full Confederate uniform, has been glimpsed in Bellevue's ballroom, sometimes in the company of his young lady. Over at Smith Hall, now an administration building at LaGrange College, a Southern cavalry officer has been spotted wandering around the second floor. An unseen but still sensed spirit searches the building, calling "Lorena" in a soft male voice. Women have even felt a ghostly touch on their arms as Griffin continues to seek his love. Smith Hall, built in 1842, is the oldest structure on campus. The four columns out front, brick covered with plaster, are named Matthew, Mark, Luke and John.

Bellevue is owned by the LaGrange Woman's Club and is open for visitation at certain times.

The story of that past, Lorena,
Alas! I care not to repeat,
The hopes that could not last, Lorena,
They lived, but only lived to cheat.
I would not cause e'en one regret
To rankle in your bosom now;
For 'if we try we may forget,'
Were words of thine long years ago.

Yes, these were words of thine, Lorena,
They burn within my memory yet;
They touched some tender chords, Lorena,
Which thrill and tremble with regret.
'Twas not thy woman's heart that spoke;
Thy heart was always true to me:
A duty, stern and pressing, broke
The tie which linked my soul with thee.

It matters little now, Lorena,
The past—is in eternal past,
Our heads will soon lie down, Lorena,
Life's tide is ebbing out so fast;
There is a future—oh, thank God—
Of life this is so small a part,
'Tis dust to dust beneath the sod,
But there, up there, 'tis heart to heart.

Is That You, Samuel?

When Ghost Force investigated a haunted house in LaGrange, it reported that one member "saw a full bodied apparition of a Confederate soldier in a gray uniform and cap, with a black bushy beard, standing at the top of the stairs looking at her" as she prepared to snap a picture. The member dubbed the figure "Samuel." The photo shows an outline of the image with three orbs. Light bulbs around the house are known to burn out unusually fast.

Ghost Force visited the LaGrange Confederate Cemetery on the night of January 24, 2004, tracking paranormal activity with Tri-Field Natural EM meters and dowsing rods and snapping away with cameras to capture orbs. The meter and rods "were going crazy," the team reported, and a red vortex was captured near a gnarled tree. In the cemetery, a member named Carol was utilizing dowsing rods that "went crazy as she was talking to the spirits," their website stated. She also took a roll of photos, and only one was blurred. "The apparition coming out of the ground bottom left," the report continued, "streaking Orbs/Ecto, and other faces in the picture speak for themselves."

COLUMBUS

Columbus was one of the Confederacy's most important industrial centers, but it did not feel the hard hand of war until the very end. Perhaps as a result, this seems to be the least haunted city in the state. However, on River Walk, people experience cold spots and hear voices of spirits strolling along the Chattahoochee. Legend holds that they are Confederate soldiers and their dance partners taking a midnight walk.

National Civil War Naval Museum at Port Columbus

The National Civil War Naval Museum tells vital stories of America's Civil War naval history. During the war, Columbus produced a powerful ironclad ram, the CSS *Jackson*. Progress on the ironclad was slow. It had been launched but not yet commissioned when Union general James Wilson captured Columbus in April 1865.

Downstream at Saffold, a wooden gunboat, the CSS *Chattahoochee*, was constructed. The *Chattahoochee* was deployed downstream to the Apalachicola River to protect the Chattahoochee River and Columbus, but on an expedition, a boiler exploded, killing and wounding a number of men. The ship was taken up the river to Columbus for repairs.

General Wilson fired both warships and set them adrift. They burned to the waterline and sank below the city.

During the centennial of the Civil War, cofferdams were constructed around the hulks, the water within was pumped out, and the ships were extricated from the mud and returned to Columbus, where they were displayed under open sheds. The hulls deteriorated from moisture and humidity until this outstanding facility was constructed in 2000 to display the *Jackson* and *Chattahoochee*. Besides the ships, the museum has dozens of models of ironclads, a number of flags and many other artifacts and a replica of a Confederate ironclad inside and a full-scale Confederate gunboat—the *Water Witch*—outside.

It was not long after the dedication that a spirit, presumably related to the *Chattahoochee*'s fatal accident, appeared.

One day, a lone shopper was browsing in the large gift shop when she was struck in the back, squarely between the shoulders, by a book. She quickly looked around but found she was alone. She spotted Jerry Franklin, maintenance supervisor of the museum, standing by the entrance. All he could do was shrug his shoulders, as if to say, "Just another day at the haunted naval museum."

The book used to assault the visitor was the *Confederate Navy: The Ships, Men, and Organization 1861–1865*. The book had been so violently handled that its spine had been torn and broken. Lane Palmer, a teacher and museum volunteer, purchased this evidence of paranormal activity.

Some volumes from a bookshelf on the back wall are propelled up to seven feet and some land upright, as if a considerate ghost had carefully set them on the floor.

"This happens all the time," commented Susan Ingram, manager of visitor services. Generally, every two weeks a book is lofted by invisible hands. "It kind of goes in cycles," she added. She and staffer Leslie have witnessed flying books, books piled on the floor in the morning and books fallen off shelves during the day.

On the front counter is a square black spindle, holding pins, key rings and whistles that can be spun by hand. On a number of occasions, the spindle starts spinning with no human touch and when there is not a whisper of air current in the gift shop.

Although Bruce Smith, the museum's executive director, did not claim his museum was haunted, he did tell Tim Chitwood of the *Columbus Ledger-Enquirer* in August 2009, "I am prepared to say that we have these continued unexplainable dumping of books on the floor. We didn't know what the deal was. We've looked, and we can't figure it out. We think we've got these things anchored pretty good, and the next thing we know, crash! And there's nobody in the store."

These and other reported phenomena, including footsteps heard aboard the *Jackson*—which is suspended above the floor and inaccessible to visitors—and voices heard from deep within the deserted museum, have been going on for years. It is thought that a phantom sailor apparition had been caught on the surveillance system.

In response to the newspaper article, a volunteer from the earlier facility commented that the ghost: "was never violent back then. He liked to mess with things…I wonder why he is so upset? His [favorite] thing to do when I was there was mess with the boat in the aquarium and make it splash around!"

The museum has sponsored a ghost tour and invited paranormal investigators to practice their craft. On the night of May 22, 2010, a team from the Ghosts of Georgia Paranormal Investigations gathered at the naval museum for an evening of ghost hunting. Eleven people were present to investigate stories of paranormal events reported by visitors and staff. Claims included "books flying off shelves in the store, footsteps on the *Jackson*, disembodied voices, unknown tapping sounds, sound of a bell clanking, sound of a horn, a person's shoulder jerked, and a girl felt tugging on her pants."

In the Jackson Room were heard "what sounded like a lot of running back and forth across the ship." Members repeatedly asked if an entity was causing the noise, and the response was always two knocks for yes. A flashlight turned on and off, and at one point two members "saw something or someone standing on the ship." A second stint in the Jackson Room "saw someone walking across the room." There were two temperature drops, one of fifteen degrees, the other of ten degrees, and a flashlight repeatedly activated.

In the Chattahoochee Room, the temperature dropped nine degrees, and two people felt dizzy as if on a rocking ship.

Aboard a mock-up of the USS *Hartford*, audio phenomena was common—a foghorn, four footsteps, a scuffing chair and tapping and banging from two different locations were heard. One investigator was touched twice and felt uneasy.

An investigator in the theater "could smell ocean water extremely well."

The summary stated that every investigator experienced at least one unexplained occurrence, most of them verifying staff reports. Office lights turned on, temperatures dropped and knocking and EVPs were recorded in response to questions. The organization found both intelligent and residual haunting and declared the site "very active and definitely haunted!"

Effigy Paranormal had reached the same conclusion after their November 20, 2009 investigation. As they sat in the Ward Room of the *Hartford*, one saw something moving as another felt something brush through her hair, and a medium felt something brush her cheek. At the same moment, a museum employee had chest pain and trouble breathing. The employee rushed from the room. At that moment an EMF meter spiked at 7.5. Effigy Paranormal considered the physical manifestations experienced and the EMF reading to be "true documentation" of paranormal activity.

The Alabama Paranormal Research Team arrived to evaluate the facility on August 15, 2009, staying eight hours, from 7:00 p.m. to 3:00 a.m. The group's leader, Faith Serafin of Salem, Alabama, said the ghost hunt vastly "exceeded [her] expectations," with more recordable EVPs than any site in her experience, including many "platinum EVPs" of three obviously different voices and personalities that haunt the museum. EVPs included "Sit down," "Hey, Mark," "Argh" (obviously from a deceased pirate) and most spooky, "Would like coffee (or coffin)." Serafin noted a "wealth of personal experiences" by most of the staff and team members.

At one point, they were standing outside the Jackson Room when all heard the sound of hard-soled footsteps walking on wood. The steps ceased when Serafin asked who was there.

As the team gathered around a table in the *Hartford* all but one member "felt something brush past them or stroke them…as if it just went in a circle around the table," stated Serafin. An EVP said, "Sit down."

In summary, Serafin said, "There is no doubt in my mind that there are still some sailors at Port Columbus." She added that "it was almost as if the entities present were in direct communication with us at almost every moment inside Port Columbus."

The Alabama Paranormal Research Team returned in January 2012, when they encountered an "abundance of EVP's and personal

Employees, visitors and ghost hunters alike have heard deceased sailors pacing abroad the CSS *Jackson*, and shadowy guards still protect the hull.

observations," particularly in the Jackson Room, where several observed movement on the ship and around the room. "Shadows of what appeared to be legs, walked alongside the opposite side of the ship," the Team reported, and they heard something "dragging and banging" loud enough to be taped. EVPs included "Shhhh," "Ha, ha, ha, ha" and "You're not scary." Aboard the *Hartford*, EVPs stated, "Right now! Right now!" and "No, do what Faith says," the latter an apparent reference to the group's leader.

Serafin is author of *Haunted Columbus, Georgia: Phantoms of the Fountain City.*

Crybaby Bridge

One of Georgia's most haunted locations is Crybaby Bridge, located north of Columbus on Old Whitesville Road. Jan Doolittle Page, who operates a website that documents historic and interesting sites in western Georgia, received an e-mail from a woman relating an experience she had in the 1960s. She and a friend were driving down Old Whitesville

Road when they "saw a man leaning against a tree; his back was against the tree, and it appeared he had one leg drawn up with his foot against the tree. She said she thought she saw bloody rags on them. He nodded as they passed." Afterward, she "realized he was wearing what appeared to be a Confederate uniform and that his leg was not behind him but was missing."

Jan was reminded of this tale when she received a message from Christine, who lives near Old Whitesville Road. As Christine and a friend drove down the road one day, they "saw a guy hobbling across the road. We thought that he was a real person until we got closer to him. I could tell that he was dressed in gray, and he seemed to be missing a leg. He stopped at the other side, and when we got up to where we should have been able to pull up near him, there was no one there. We think maybe he was a Civil War soldier."

AMERICUS

The Garden Inn Bed-and-Breakfast

On December 18, 1846, James K. Daniel purchased twenty-one acres on what is now Rees Park and constructed his house three years later. In October 1994, the private home was purchased by Donald and Jodi Miles and converted into a bed-and-breakfast. The Americus Garden Inn was purchased by Kim and Susan Egelseer in 2002.

The Egelseers believe the inn is home to what they consider to be "a warm presence," a friendly ghost. This spirit manifests itself in typical paranormal fashion, as the scent of a woman's perfume in guestrooms late in the evening; footsteps pacing through unoccupied rooms; doors creaking open without motivation; clock radios switching themselves on and off; and objects like keys being shifted from place to place. The Egelseers have evidence of paranormal activity on film and audio tape, as do many guests. They call their primary ghost Isabella.

Previous tenants had lost a daughter in a car accident. When they heard footsteps overhead at night, the parents took comfort in the sound, believing that their girl had come home to them in the only way she could.

A Night at the Inn

Having heard ghost stories of this inn, Earline and I booked the Veranda Room for a night. Among the assortment of games available was an Ouija board, but no one, including us, had the nerve to try it out.

Susan knew I wanted to hear ghost stories, so she began relating her many experiences soon after she greeted us. We had spent only two minutes at the inn when Susan introduced us to Josh, who was honeymooning in the Scarlett Room with his new bride.

"We were in bed last night around eleven," Josh immediately started, "and I heard a man's boot hit the floor right outside our room. I heard a click, like a key opening an old fashioned spring lock, then a door opening and closing." He explained that carpet covered the hallway, but he plainly heard the boot strike wood and not carpet. When he added that he thought everyone else on the floor was asleep, Susan interjected, "You two were the only ones in the house at that time last night."

At one point, she paused, bade a passing couple hello and waited until they entered the parlor and the wife started playing the piano. Quietly, Susan said, "That couple is really religious and they don't want to hear about the ghosts." Later, Susan came up to us and said, "You remember the couple that didn't want to hear about ghosts? They just told me that when they went to light candles in the parlor for reading the Bible, they couldn't find their matches." The ghost had struck again, and all three of us laughed.

"I have only seen one actual ghost, a full-bodied apparition," Susan said. "I was outside on the second-floor balcony, just enjoying the breeze and the view. I had a feeling that I should turn to the left, and I saw a man standing there. I was startled by the sight but not frightened. I saw that he was wearing a uniform—the coat was double breasted, with two rows of gold buttons and a yellow sash. He didn't notice me; he didn't interact with me. He was living in his own world. He stood there, solid and real, for just a moment before fading away."

Records of the solider, a son of the builder, prove that in early 1865, he was stationed in Americus as a quartermaster, most likely working for the notorious prison camp at Andersonville.

"It seems as though he has refused to leave and keeps watch over the house even now," Susan explained. She continued:

Things always happen to the self-professed nonbelievers. One man told me he didn't believe all of the weird stories. He was a jogger, and it being August in the deep South, he took a run early in the morning through Oak Grove Cemetery, which is nearby, paved, pleasant, with no traffic. When he returned, he said he had seen something kind of strange. He had seen a homeless man there wearing a coat. I said, "Are you sure he was wearing a coat?"

"Yes, why?"

"It's August in Americus, Georgia."

He paused thoughtfully. I asked what part of the cemetery he was in, "Was it near the Confederate section?" He replied that it was.

The figure had simply "disappeared."

When we entered our room, Earline flicked the switch on the wall for the five-globe light fixture. Nothing happened. She then pulled the cord attached to the lights, but the lights refused to come on. I also tried it unsuccessfully. We left for supper, and upon our return, we both again failed to activate the lights.

Susan stopped by to tell us about breakfast the next morning, and we told her about the problem with the lights. "Oh," she said, "flip this switch, then pull the cord," and she wed actions to words. Still nothing happened. After a moment, Susan said aloud, "Excuse me, but we need the lights." For a second, I was puzzled by her statement and then realized she was addressing Isabella. Susan again flipped the switch and pulled the cord and light flooded the room. "Thank you," Susan politely said to the air. To me and Earline, she said "Isabella was just saying hello."

Before leaving, Susan told us a story about our room:

After two ladies spent the night in the Veranda Room, they checked out and said they had thoroughly enjoyed their stay. Later, when I went to clean the room, I found four chairs jammed up against the closet door. The women had pushed the two room chairs against the door, then went out into the hall and brought in two others, and carefully pushed all four against the closet door. This intrigued me, so I gave them enough time to get home and gave them a call.

"I'm not upset about it," I said, "but I just have to know. Why did you push four chairs up against the closet door?"

The lady was quiet a minute and then said, "It was the only way we could keep Isabella in the closet. That door kept opening, and we kept

A Confederate soldier, once a resident of the Americus Garden Inn, has been sighted on an upstairs balcony, and "Isabella" cannot be contained in this closet.

closing it firmly. But it would just suddenly make a sound, and the door would open purposefully. We'll be back," she promised, "but we want a different room next time."

"Have a pleasant evening," Susan said, smiled and left.

We kept a close watch on that closet door, but Isabella gave us a quiet night.

Susan shared other ghost stories about the inn, such as one incident that occurred shortly after the purchase of the inn.

The first thing that vanished after hers and Kim's arrival was a plain cookie sheet, and Susan could not imagine why anyone would steal such a worthless object. She and Kim emptied the kitchen cabinet to no avail. Several weeks later, the cookie sheet appeared in an obvious place where it could never have been overlooked.

Susan is convinced that one spirit in the house is a child, probably a girl because the things she does are innocent pranks or just the behavior typical of a child.

"Our ghost is a warm presence," as Susan likes to call it. "Never threatening or scary. It quietly shares our house." She shared another story of one of these pranks:

A girl working for Habitat for Humanity had her parents in and put them up here while they visited. They didn't believe the stories. One night as they lay in bed, they heard something drop inside a drawer. I asked if they had looked in the drawers, and they said, "No, and we don't intend to." They left for an outing, and I went in to clear their room. I was curious even if they weren't, so I opened the drawers. Inside one I found several chocolate kisses that sit on a saucer beside the bed. When they returned, I told them that was a funny prank they had played on me. Their reaction was blank puzzlement. I decided they probably didn't want to hear about what really happened, so I smiled and said, "Never mind."

More than just a prank-playing child seems to be in some of the rooms, however:

Another unbeliever approached me one morning with his wife. He also wanted to tell me something but was reluctant to do so. I asked if there was a problem with the room that I could help them with. He demurred, but his wife finally said, "Hank, you saw it. Tell her."

Finally Hank started, "I woke up suddenly about 1:00 a.m., and there was a man in the bed with us. He was sleeping between me and my wife." I asked him to describe the man, but he said he thought it was best to ignore the situation and rolled over and went back to sleep. He was really disturbed by the incident.

In 2007, Americus was struck by a devastating tornado that took lives and caused extensive property damage, including the destruction of the hospital. The Garden Inn lost thirty pecan trees, and only a newly installed back porch saved the historic home from destruction. Susan and Kim have worked tirelessly to repair the house and grounds, and so far, the paranormal activity has largely ceased, as if the spirits are sympathetic and appreciate their efforts to protect their home.

JACKSONVILLE

The Soldier Who Returned

Professor Robert Jefferies of LaGrange College related a childhood experience to Julian Williams, a historian of the tiny community of Jacksonville, Georgia, located along the Ocmulgee River in central Georgia. Jefferies's grandmother Annie Jane White Wells was dying in 1939. Her Confederate veteran husband, Sergeant Newton R. Wells of the Fiftieth Georgia Infantry, had passed away years earlier, in 1911. While the family gathered around Miss Annie's bed, Robert and his brother were playing outside. Looking at a field beyond the yard, they saw a tree with a swing hanging from a branch, "and in that swing was a beautiful young lady dressed in the attire of the Civil War era," Williams wrote. "Not only was there a young lady in the swing but [also] by her side helping her swing was a Confederate soldier who had come across the field to join her at the tree!"

Robert ran inside to tell the family about the sight. His mother returned with him, but the tree had no swing and there was no trace of the gay young couple. As they scanned the field, someone left the house to tell them that Annie had crossed over Jordan to Beulahland. According to Williams, Jefferies ran this scenario through his head countless times and "concluded that perhaps he was given the chance to see a scene from the past—when the young girl, his grandmother, was swinging in the swing, and her Confederate suitor, destined to become her husband, home from the Civil War, joined her there. And now he had come back one last time, from his own death years before, to escort his precious love to those happy regions beyond that veil we cannot comprehend."

Irwin County

Ghosts Generated by the Last Act of the War

When Robert E. Lee abandoned Petersburg and started toward his fate at Appomattox Court House, the Confederate government abandoned Richmond and started south in an attempt to reach the Trans-Mississippi or a foreign sanctuary. President Jefferson Davis traveled through the Carolinas and crossed the Savannah River into Georgia, dissolving the government at Washington on May 5. Davis, his family and a small escort camped on the night of May 9 near the village of Irwinville. During the night, two different units of Federal cavalry found the camp, and at dawn, they attacked. The surprised Confederates offered no resistance, but in the early morning darkness, a spirited skirmish broke out between the two Union commands, each believing the other to be Davis's guard. Two Northern soldiers died before the tragic mistake was realized. They were the last casualties of the Civil War, today buried at Andersonville National Cemetery.

The site of Jefferson Davis's capture is now a historic park. A museum displays relics, including part of a tree that stood where Davis was seized, and a memorial topped by a bronze bust of the Confederate president marks the exact spot of his capture. The site of the skirmish is preserved. A posting on a Georgia State Parks and Historic Sites website suggested the little park was haunted, stating, "Some still believe those soldiers haunt the grounds, perhaps trying to find each other for forgiveness. In the middle of the night, one could possibly encounter approaching footsteps despite no living person walking nearby or jump at the sound of mysterious gunfire in the distance. Are these happenings a result of a wayward small animal or the ghost of a lost Union soul? We are left to wonder. Believe what you will!" So I decided to check out the stories.

The spirit of a Confederate officer appeared to the owner of the Americus Garden Inn on the upstairs porch.

"Before we moved in here a lot of the locals would come in and they would always tell me, 'This was a haunted place to work,'" said Daniel Gray, site manager at the park and a native of Cedartown.

One night in early 2005, after several hours of sleep, Gray said, "My wife woke me up, and she said there's a gunshot in the park." Alarmed, he threw on his uniform, grabbed a flashlight and slipped outside. By security light, he saw no cars in the parking lot. "I listened, and the dogs were all asleep," Gray continued, "and that's weird because they bark when they hear something." Gray found no evidence of intruders and the couple returned to bed, his wife saying, "'I know what I heard—a gunshot.' I said, 'I'm sure you did.'" Several nights later she woke him again, saying, "I heard gunshots," only this time there were multiple reports. Gray again searched the grounds but found nothing.

A month later, Gray's mother-in-law spent the night. "We got up in the morning and we're drinking our coffee, sitting around watching TV and she said, 'Y'all don't laugh at me, but I woke up last night and jumped up out of that bed. I heard gunshots, and when I heard it again, it came from the other side of the park,'" several hundred yards distant, where the skirmish occurred, an incident of which she was unaware. She spent one more night with the Grays, and again she couldn't sleep. "Every time I fell asleep, I could hear gunshots," she swore.

For some unknown reason, Gray said, "I've never heard the gunshots. It's weird—I wish I could have heard the shots."

"We had a ranger who worked here in the past that always heard someone walking in the museum," Gray related. "She always joked that it was Jefferson Davis. She looked around the museum to see where the footsteps were coming from." Not only was the museum empty, but also "there was no one in the park" at that time.

VALDOSTA

A Confederate Ghost in Very South Central Georgia

It was late on the night of July 9, 2007, in Valdosta, and fifteen-year-old Laura Gagne was relaxing on her bed watching television. Around 12:30 a.m., she was startled by "an aggressive pound on [her] bedroom floor." She was frightened for fifteen minutes, she wrote in Archives X, and "held [her] breath and tried not to move." The fear passed as she was caught up in a TV program. Then she "could barely hear a cabinet open and closing," which occurred every thirty seconds. She said, "There was something in my house that didn't want us to hear, or was trying to tell us something." Laura turned off the TV to listen. She said she tried to "figure out where they were from but I couldn't. They soon stopped, and I rolled over to go to sleep." She was nearly asleep when, she said, "I heard a shuffle of feet across my carpet, and I was wide awake again and for the rest of the night." Her nine-year-old sister "told [her] that she was looking into the hallway from her bed and saw someone run past her door." It was a young man wearing a uniform, prompting Laura to write, "I think we came in contact with a ghost from the Civil War," who apparently had a female companion. Several nights earlier, the sister "had seen a shadow of a woman on the hallway wall."

PART IV

ANDERSONVILLE

Hell on Earth and in the Hereafter

ANDERSONVILLE PRISON AND CEMETERY

I spent my last two years of college at Georgia Southwestern College in Americus, a good little school and a fine small city. I remained in Americus for my first year of teaching in Macon County. Every time I drove home from school and each day I worked in Montezuma, I twice passed Andersonville National Cemetery and Prison, the thirteen thousand graves plainly visible behind the low stone wall. When I first moved to Americus, I often visited the cemetery. I would cruise through the serene landscaped cemetery and then drive a short distance to the prison site, a stark, barren area surrounded by a perimeter road and dominated by elevations topped with earthworks that once held batteries of artillery, ready in 1864 to spew canister into escaping prisoners. Perhaps it is the knowledge of how forty-five thousand men suffered and the deaths of thirteen thousand of them that make the prison site oppressive. Or perhaps it is the spirits of those many souls that still cannot escape the hell that was Andersonville. If any place in U.S. Civil War history should be haunted, this is it. Not Gettysburg, where free men fought and died on their own terms, but this truly godforsaken plain, where desperate, hopeless men quietly succumbed to hunger, disease and exposure. It does not require much imagination to envision horrific scenes of gaunt, emaciated, living skeletons, much less their spirits.

I have heard stories of Andersonville's ghosts for forty years, particularly tableaus of the Raiders being hanged and the spirit of Henry Wirz,

This statue at Andersonville illustrates the terrible conditions under which forty-five thousand Union soldiers lived.

commandant of the prison, stalking the grounds. As feature editor of the *Sou'wester* (no kidding, that was Southwestern's college paper; we were also the 'Canes, for Hurricanes), I drove to Andersonville late one night and slowly drove back and forth on Georgia 49 in front of the cemetery. I have honestly forgotten whether I saw something or I merely wanted to, but I returned to the dorm, sat down in front of my trusty Royal manual and clacked out a story about Wirz's return—a dejected specter pleading for forgiveness and telling passersby that he had done the best he could.

The Return of Henry Wirz

Henry Wirz was an immigrant from Switzerland who settled in Kentucky to practice medicine. He joined Confederate service in 1861, lost the use of an arm in combat and had several positions within the government. Sent to command at Andersonville, he was hated by the prisoners yet did what he could to alleviate conditions. At the war's end, he was tried and convicted of murdering prisoners, although much of the testimony against him was fraudulent, and executed.

Kathryn Tucker Windham, in *13 Georgia Ghosts and Jeffrey*, tells the following story. It was nearly midnight in December 1971. A civic meeting in Americus had gone long and Louise Campbell was driving north on Georgia 49 to Montezuma, where she would drop off her friends Mr. and Mrs. Norman Gerritsen before continuing to her home in Perry.

They were passing the national cemetery when Louise spotted a man standing beside the road. He was dressed in a long, heavy military overcoat, the collar turned up against the cold, and a uniform cap covered his head. The sight made her "feel eerie and uncomfortable," she said, as if she had been transported back in time.

Mrs. Campbell immediately braked, preparing to turn around and view the figure again. As she asked if either of her friends had witnessed the sight, Norman interrupted her, saying, according to Matt Anderson, "Yes. I saw the man in the strange uniform." His wife had not but wanted to sight what had so startled the others.

Little time was lost before the car was returning south, but the man had vanished, which the two witnesses thought was as strange as the man's appearance. They were certain he could not have gotten into the woods or across the cemetery wall before they reversed their course.

Thirteen thousand Federal prisoners died at Andersonville; some of their souls have yet to find rest.

Norman said the man "had on an overcoat, a military coat of some kind, and a cap. I couldn't see the color, but the uniform looked odd and old, like it might have come out of the Civil War period."

He suggested it had been a ghost, and Louise said, "I agree with you. We both saw it—or him—standing right there and now the figure has gone. Vanished."

They speculated about the soldier's identity on the ride home and discussed the incident with friends. There was no reason not to believe Louise and Norman, so discussion shifted to who the figure might have been. There are plenty of candidates—any of the thirteen thousand souls laid to unrest behind that fence. Perhaps it was one of the tormented Raiders, but most believed it was the spirit of Henry Wirz returned to redeem himself or explain his actions. Another reported story has the Wirz ghost offering food and drink to equally spectral prisoners.

Wirz was hanged long ago and far away, in November 1865, at Old Capital Prison in Washington, D.C. In July 2000, I located his grave in Mount Olivet Cemetery in D.C., marked by a simple stone. It took considerable effort to find. I wondered if he was yet at peace or if thirteen thousand souls would haunt him forever.

For some years, Andersonville had what is called a "truck-drivers phenomenon." The site is located at a sharp bend in a busy highway, and tractor-trailer drivers often reported figures clad in Confederate uniforms that suddenly appeared beside the road, causing them to brake to screeching halts.

The Fog of Souls

Gene Harmon, a reenactor with the 123rd New York Volunteer Infantry, Company D (which also portrays a Confederate unit), says you can experience strange things at Andersonville even at high noon.

"You feel a coldness," Harmon told Jeff Belanger in *Ghosts of War*. "You'll be standing there, and it'll be just like you walked into a freezer. Your bones will hurt from the cold." But the effect gives way to warmth just a few feet away. "Or you'll be standing there and you feel a breeze but there's no breeze blowing anywhere. Or you'll hear noises."

Harmon's unit members spent the weekend of March 10–11, 2001, portraying Union prisoners held at Andersonville, where members of the original Civil War unit were imprisoned. At least one died and was buried there.

Darkness had fallen, but a full moon illuminated the prison site when Harmon and four comrades decided to walk to Providence Spring from the reconstructed portion of the stockade where they were camped. They took pictures of themselves at the spring and then stood around quietly talking and looking over the site of the prison. They watched as a fog slowly rolled in and started to walk through it toward the end of the prison site.

"[The fog] seemed to quickly swirl around us along with a sudden drop in temperature," Harmon wrote. "It was a cool night, but we found ourselves shivering and blowing in our hands to warm them up."

The fog partially obscured "dark forms," which turned out to be trees and bushes. As the group continued their hike, "a couple of dark forms were noticed further up the hillside" at a corner of the stockade. Realizing that they had left the fog, they turned around to look at it, but "there wasn't any," and the men were "still cold—like ice." When they reached the corner, nothing was found that could have shaped the "dark forms" they had observed earlier. "What were the other dark forms we saw?" Harmon wrote. "Who knows."

The reenactors watched the distant campfires reflecting off the reconstructed stockade before retracing their steps. In the ravine, "the fog rose from the ground all around us almost instantly." The men "brusquely walked through and started up the opposite slope. As we started up again, the fog instantly vanished!"

Harmon and one friend decided to see if the fog would repeat its trick and returned to the gully, followed by their cursing colleagues who would not let their buddies go alone. The fog "seemed to part and withdraw away from us," and "once again the fog just vanished." Stepping onto the perimeter road, "the iciness disappeared as well…a very discernible increase in the temperature."

They observed the bottom for a while, but the fog did not return. Harmon suggested walking into the valley again, but his friends understandably threatened to kick his butt if he attempted it.

"The ghosts of Andersonville had welcomed us as some of their own," Harmon believed. "Their presence was felt in the fog and the far end of the stockade. The iciness pronouncing their close proximity, but never once feeling a sense of foreboding or ill will. How different it might have been had we been wearing gray."

On another occasion Harmon and several friends, including a woman, left camp during the night and "went down to the creek down there and we crossed over until we were walking along the bottom land," Harman told writer Jeff Belanger. "We got up on the road and the lady with me turned and said, 'Hey did you see him?' And I said, 'Did I see what?' She said there was a guy walking with us back there. Well there wasn't anybody back there—it was just me and her."

Scents and Sounds of the Past

In *Civil War Ghosts and Legends*, Nancy Roberts tells the story of two friends—Bill Blue, a native Southerner, and Currie McClellan, a Vietnam veteran of Northern descent whose great-great-grandfather had languished at Andersonville.

In July 1990, the pair briefly explored the village of Andersonville, where prisoners disembarked from trains and continued to the prison. They argued, as friends do, over whether Confederate mistreatment or

Federal prisoner exchange policy was responsible for the horrors that occurred at this site.

Blue and McClellan drove into Americus to eat supper in the Victorian splendor of the restored Windsor Hotel (talk about haunted places—I toured the then derelict structure as a student), then returned to Andersonville and parked their van in a parking area across the highway from the entrance to the cemetery.

They continued the tense conversation as they crossed the road and entered the cemetery. The graves of the Raiders, separated from the others, are located not far inside the grounds. The friends discussed the fate of the Raiders, and McClellan spit on the grave of the renegades' leader, declaring his hatred for soldiers guilty of murdering and stealing from their fellow prisoners. "Damn their souls!" he declared. "Hell's fire is too good for them."

Blue and McClellan inflated air mattresses and slept in the van, McClellan feeling disquieted. A little after midnight, he woke to find the air permeated with a strong unpleasant odor. He opened the van's side door and nearly gagged. The overpowering smell was a combination of massed unwashed bodies, raw sewage and rotting flesh.

Six Raiders robbed and killed fellow soldiers. Visitors who curse them receive nocturnal visits from their spirits.

By now Blue was up, awakened by the penetrating stench. As they attempted to divine its origin, they heard a low chorus of male voices growing stronger and stronger. "We shouldn't have camped near a graveyard," Blue joked, but he fetched a shotgun from the van. McClellan suggested that the sound was distant thunder, but Blue distinguished a word. The ethereal chorus was shouting "Wil-lee, Wil-lee, Wil-lee," the name of the Raiders' leader. Then he heard a single, low, slow eerie voice responding, "Had to rob them. Couldn't have survived otherwise."

McClellan was unable to distinguish the words, but Blue heard the loud chant change to "Hang them! Hang them! Hang them!" The voices grew thunderously loud, then peaked and quickly faded away as did the horrible smell, although the odor seemed to cling to the earth.

Blue and McClellan considered the mystery from all angles. One suggested that the odor had originated from a factory, and in fact, a large pulpwood plant is located barely five miles away between Andersonville and Montezuma. However, as a lifelong Southerner, I can testify that pulpwood stink is not as bad as it used to be and never dissipates quickly. Then one of the men realized that the date was July 11, the day the Raiders were executed. On the following morning, park workers said they had never heard (or smelled) such a circumstance on any previous July 11 or any other date.

"Some of the kids think the ghost of Wirz still walks the road out there," a ranger told them. "Comes back because he feels guilty, I guess."

Dead Man's Walk

Blue & Gray magazine related a similar story. In their tale, two men toured the prison and cemetery late in the day. One of them spat on Willie Collins's grave as he cursed the executed Raiders. These history enthusiasts also camped out near the prison. Soon after their campfire died down, they heard slow, heavy footsteps approaching them up a gravel drive. The men rolled out of their sleeping bags to investigate but found no prowler. As soon as they settled down, the sound started again, this time around their campsite. They shouted in the direction of the footfalls, but that provoked no change in the slow, methodical, ponderous steps. Spooked, the men hastily packed up long before daybreak and fled the scene. They have assured other Civil War travelers that they would never taunt the dead again, for a Raider certainly seemed to stalk them from the grave.

Sky Pilot

There was little noble about Andersonville Prison, but Father Whelan, a Catholic priest, provided a spot of humanity and decency. Andersonville lacked a chaplain, a deficiency noted by a passing Protestant minister. He alerted the bishop of Savannah, who dispatched Father Whelan, a priest who had previously ministered to the Confederate garrison of Fort Pulaski. He arrived on June 16, 1864, and was appalled by the barbaric conditions he found in the camp.

Father Whelan did what he could to materially help the suffering, bringing food and borrowing money to purchase flour so patients in the hospital could have bread. Mostly he brought comfort to the large numbers of Catholic prisoners, listening to their fears, hearing their confessions and, too often, administering last rites.

Father Whelan rose early every morning in the shack he slept in near Andersonville, said his prayers and walked to the prison, where he stayed until late in the evening. He ate little better than the prisoners and risked his life constantly, ministering among the diseased men in a filthy environment.

Other men of the cloth came to Andersonville but were soon repelled by the circumstances. Father Whelan stayed until the end, a true servant of God who believed that every man, even the enemy, was his brother.

In *Georgia Ghosts*, Nancy Roberts tells of Robert Berry, a historian who wrote his master's thesis on Andersonville Prison. Near dark one evening, he left the prison site on foot, walking to the nearby village of Andersonville. His mind was preoccupied with the overwhelming feeling of sadness that affects visitors to this notorious place of misery.

A strange looking person ahead of him, an awkward looking figure dressed in black, diverted Berry's attention. The misshapen fellow had extremely long arms, a short body, and a large head. Most curiously, the fellow held an opened umbrella over his head although it was not raining or sunny.

Berry then detected a nasty odor that had no obvious source. He passed the curious little man who had fallen to his knees along the roadside, as if in prayer or searching the grass for a lost possession. Berry thought that odd but continued walking.

A little farther along his journey, the horrid scent engulfed him again. Berry looked around and saw nothing—even the weird man had disappeared. He picked up his pace until he was running in an effort to elude the odor. Out of breath, he finally stopped. Seconds later a voice behind Berry said, "My dear man." He whirled around to find the figure in black staring intently at his face. "I am ready to give you the last rites."

In a flash, Berry realized who the man was: Father Whelan. The figure had wild features and still held the unfurled umbrella. Terrified, Berry sprinted for his car and drove away as quickly as he could. He slept little that night and returned to the museum in the morning.

"I would guess that you met Father Whelan," an employee revealed. Occasionally a visitor reported seeing the same strange man that had frightened Berry, complete with umbrella and black clothing. Berry asked about the umbrella.

"The summer sun beat down with such intensity that Father Whelan always held an umbrella over his head," the park employee said. "I don't believe in ghosts," he said but continued, "I know it's Father Whelan."

Ian Alan elaborated on Father Whelan in *Georgia Ghosts: They Are Among Us*. He has Father Charlie Martin, a disgruntled priest from Atlanta, visiting Andersonville in a distraught state. Reflecting on his situation, he sat on a bench, where he was approached by an older priest sporting a large umbrella. He listened to the young priest's position, attempting to encourage him, but grew impatient as Martin expressed selfishness and indulgences. The older priest asked how many confessions he heard a day or last rites he administered on a daily basis. The young man soon detected the stench of death and felt the presence of many miserable souls. Suddenly, he saw the Andersonville of 1864 as the damned soldiers pressed against him. Martin abruptly snapped back to modern reality to find a groundskeeper enquiring about his health. When Martin described his experience, the worker grinned and said, "You've just met Father Whelan. He came to the prison in 1864, and some say he never left." Employees encountered him on occasion, the man explained, and the ghost still seeks out those who need him.

Jeff Belanger believes Father Peter Whelan is often seen at the cemetery wall along Georgia 49.

Experiences of Reenactors

Andersonville now hosts two highly publicized and well-attended reenactment weekends a year, in the spring and fall. Reenactor "Mike" camped in the village near the cemetery, where some Confederate guards who died at the prison were originally buried. For two nights, he said, "Around 1:00 a.m. both nights I would awaken with the hair on my neck standing up."

Another Confederate reenactor reported that during a visit to the Drummer Boy Museum in the village of Andersonville a woman entered and described an incident she and her husband experienced the previous year. As they drove out of the cemetery the woman spotted a man standing beside one of the graves. What was unusual was that he had only one leg, leaned on a crutch and wore a Confederate uniform. The wife pointed out the figure to her husband, who was driving. After they passed, the husband glanced in the rearview mirror but the figure had vanished.

Ed Crowe and fellow reenactors camped at Andersonville in August 1984. Throughout the night, all experienced "uncanny chills and sudden illnesses." They also "felt a sudden urge to leave" and did so before dawn arrived.

Another reenactor with the designation Mtuba3 has spent nights near Andersonville, writing, "Sometimes it sounds like you can still hear the moaning of the prisoners."

An Employee's Tale

John McKay is a Civil War historian who expressed amazement by "the number of serious, well-educated people who shyly bring up the subject" of Civil War ghosts. He told *Atlanta Constitution* columnist Colin Campbell that a young park ranger at Andersonville hesitantly broached the subject and then eagerly started relating stories when McKay expressed an interest. The ghosts "have been around since anyone can remember," she said. The woman concluded with a recent tale from a colleague. "It was closing time and the ranger was shooing everybody out when she spotted a man on the brick wall around the old cemetery." Some Confederate guards were originally buried on the other side of the wall (they were reburied in a special section of the Americus city cemetery later), "so it must have been one of them," she concluded.

"Whenever I talk to reenactors or historians," Campbell wrote, "the subject of ghosts comes up—combat sounds, Rebel yells and, most interesting of all, 'extra men' showing up on videos of reenactments."

For twenty years, Kevin Frye has resided near Andersonville, where he offers a service to descendants of Andersonville prisoners who live far away. He will look up and confirm the names of prisoners and then go to the cemetery and photograph individual grave markers. He has spent much time at the cemetery and prison site, and at midnight, he feels a "totally different feeling" that he describes as "unsettling...I think it's more of an aura that I feel," he told Jeff Belanger.

His biggest problem concerns the failure of his digital camera when he is attempting to photograph a gravestone, a common paranormal experience. Although he claims that he neither believes nor disbelieves in ghosts, "I'll say out loud, 'I just wanna take a couple, now,'" he said in *Ghosts of War*. As usually occurs in these instances, the camera then functions perfectly.

A visitor told Frye that while she walked near the center of the prison at the hilltop, "in her head she heard a voice say something." Looking about, she saw no one but then concentrated and thought, "Were you a prisoner here?" Receiving an affirmative reply, she asked if he had died. "Yes," was the response. She then asked for its name and received it. After looking up the name, Frye confirmed that such a man had been imprisoned at Andersonville and died there.

Star Fort Defender

Angie Madden was with a party of ghost hunters at Andersonville when she felt drawn to the Star Fort. At the entrance bridge, she noted the loud sounds of locusts, but "when I walked up the little path, everything just stopped," she told Alan Brown for *Ghost Hunters of the South*. "Dead silence. No wind, no birds, no bugs." She also said, "[I] got a warm sensation up my arms and the back of my neck." Whenever Angie focused on a cannon within the fort, "I could see something moving back and forth, like a soldier," but only when seen through the viewfinder of the camera. It was absent to the naked eye, and she repeated the experiment several dozen times. One photograph she shot showed "a real bright ball right in front of me," and as she took it, "something just took the breath away... [my] heart went up in my throat." As she turned, "I felt more warm breathing up my back. Something crossed my arms, and every little hair stood up on end. All the crickets and locusts and birds started up, and I high-tailed it down the bridge." Group members told her she was "as white as a ghost."

Providential Deliverance

Andersonville was crowded with over three times the number of men it was designed to sustain. One desperate problem was the lack of sanitary drinking water. The stockade was designed so that Sweetwater Creek flowed through the prison grounds, but unfortunately, it was fouled by swampy ground. Waste from the Confederate guard camp and cookhouse further polluted the stream, and prisoners washing in the water and using it as a toilet supplied additional filth. Drinking the contaminated water meant a slow, horrible death. Desperate prisoners dug deep wells, which unfortunately supplied only a limited amount of water.

On August 7, 8 and 9, 1864, among the hottest days at Andersonville, five hundred soldiers died. Men prayed earnestly for deliverance: God's answer was a thunderstorm of biblical proportions. Rain poured from the sky, and lightning struck in and around the prison. According to Private John Urban, the storm caused prisoners to sit on the ground and cover "their faces with their hands." The storms returned the following day, but the third dawned cool. The torrential downpours had purified Sweetwater Creek and washed much of the accumulated filth away. Also, the rains had uncovered a spring that produced plentiful fresh water for the prisoners. A more popular version of the story has divine lightning striking the very spot where the spring appeared, obviously in answer to the soldiers' devoted prayers. Whatever the source, it was immediately dubbed Providence Spring. A memorial springhouse covers this natural marvel, where the water still flows. Unfortunately, you do not want to drink the water today—it is polluted.

The Soured Ground

Early in 2001, James P. Akin, director of the International Fortean Research Society, led a team to explore Andersonville. Equipped with cameras, EMF meters and tape recorders, they noted that the landscape surrounding modern Andersonville is "the most barren area imaginable." What struck them as they approached the stockade "was that there was little wildlife noise. There were birds visible, but it appeared that none were willing to cross into the prison yard itself, especially the crows. They tended to skirt the edges of the area and stay close to the tree line." Widespread legends have crows capable of seeing "into the 'other' world and [they] are harbingers of death."

Portions of the Andersonville prison and camp have been reconstructed, showing the stockade, guard towers, dead line and primitive accommodations.

Akin rejected the idea that at Andersonville historic events are replayed "in the form of a ghostly encounter." He believes the ground there "is literally charged with negative events that took place," noting that the "ground itself will harbor no new life" other than a hardy grass. "This is soured ground. It has death written in it, and the memory of death…My theory is such that the prolonged exposure of sorrowful men baptized this ground with the unremembered tears of pain and suffering. This ground will never forget." As I said, Andersonville casts a powerfully negative spell on visitors.

As the Fortean team approached Providence Spring their "EMF meters seemed to literally bounce." The needles on two machines "buried themselves on two occasions." Akin called Providence Spring "an EMF nightmare."

The prison site "produced many strange occurrences," including "a cold spot near the Ohio memorial" that "suddenly stopped me. I felt a shiver and it passed by. The EMF meter bounced rapidly."

The IFRS group found the most activity among the trees at the northwest corner of the prison. "There were many occasions when the EMF meter would indicate something strange was nearby." Akin believed it was tied to the desperation of Federal soldiers who attempted to tunnel out of the area.

Where the remains of the excavations are today enclosed by iron fences there is "a sense of hopelessness," which he described as pervasive.

Akin noted that locals report hearing rifle fire at night and "a sound like a great tumult of people speaking all at once when the sun disappears."

Several photos revealed anomalies. One, taken at the Raiders' graves has a "long, swishing discoloration…like a washed out place on the photo." Akin reported that the "EMF meters were very active in this area."

A humanlike figure enclosed in a mist within the open area of the prison enclosure developed on one frame.

In conclusion, Akin said, "Andersonville is one of the most haunted places in the United States." He believes that "anyone who visits Andersonville prison leaves with a strong sense of sorrow" and that "the spirits of Andersonville have never left their eternal misery within the ethereal walls of this hateful place."

Another Paranormal Investigation

About half a century ago, park visitors began to report the appearance of a Federal soldier's ghost, sporting a slouch hat, leaning against a brick wall in the northwestern corner of the cemetery. Those accounts attracted the attention of the Foundation for Paranormal Research, which arrived on August 13, 2003, for a scientific explanation of this and other reported haunted places at Andersonville National Cemetery and the prison grounds.

Park rules require the presence of rangers when visitors are on the grounds, and the Park Service granted a special-use permit one day after closing hours, from 5:00 until 10:00 p.m.

"Typically, places that have experienced so much suffering and death have some sort of residual energy," Bev Greenfield, a board member, explained to reporter Sandra Powell of the *Americus Times-Recorder*. "We come with the utmost respect for that suffering. We're just trying to find out what that energy is, trying to document it."

Greenfield issued instructions to foundation members, including the admonition to treat the park with dignity. Teams were dispatched to the northwestern corner, the north gate, the interior of the stockade, monuments, collapsed escape tunnels and the reconstructed part of the wall and recreated living quarters.

Greenfield and two other members concentrated on the northwestern corner. Two of the team members, using different cameras, captured a "genuine orb" at the corner of the brick wall. "I think we very well may have captured him [the Union soldier] in these photos," she reported.

The orb moved against the wind and against gravity. A storm brewed up during the investigation, and "perhaps the electrical storm helped him to manifest that evening," Greenfield speculated. Other orbs were photographed at the Raiders' graves.

At the wall, other evidence, EVPs, were left on a digital recorder employed by Vicki Luibrand. EVPs are rarely heard on the scene "because they are at a frequency outside of normal human hearing," Luibrand stated. She is successful in 70 percent of her attempts to capture phantom mutterings.

As the three first approached the wall, investigator Donna Lynn said, "Right by the wall?" and the tape captured a male voice uttering, "Died by the wall" or "Right by the wall." These ethereal voices often seem to mimic or mock humans. The male voice then said, "Think of something you want to ask."

As they reentered their car, the recorder captured heavy male breathing, then, "Help!" and moments later, "It stinks in here," followed by coughing.

During the night, various researchers complained of extreme fatigue, nausea, pushing, heaviness and the odor of feces. On two occasions within the cemetery, dowsing rods were used successfully to communicate with spirits. One of the entities, eighteen years old, died of dysentery but reported that guards had treated him decently. He believed he was in hell and enjoyed conversing with the living. The second communication was with a twenty-one-year-old who had been shot to death.

"It seems that some [spirits] are in the present time and some are still in the past," Luibrand said. "I'm not sure if the ones from the past are still living in the past, or if we are hearing, and sometimes seeing, an imprint in time."

On several occasions, members of the Big Bend Ghost Trackers converged on Andersonville as the tourist day was ending. They split into three-person groups, each equipped with walkie-talkies, and staked out separate areas to observe. Circulating between the groups was George Fernandez, a screen writer and producer who was filming a pilot episode for a TV series.

"Intense feelings of sadness and sickness engulfed us," stated a report on their website. "The cries and pleas for mercy and help hung heavy in the atmosphere. In the cemetery area a young soldier named Owen came through during a state of meditation by one of the group's psychic investigators. Later the gravestone was discovered in the same area."

One member "experienced the feeling of being shot in the leg" near the deadline, and a guest heard footsteps behind him and a sudden coldness. When EMF meters spiked at the entrance gate, one member, an air force officer, barked orders at the "arriving" prisoners, generating greater EMF activity. Meeting inside the prison stockade, they "all felt the energies and all the emotions that went with them."

When the Atlanta Ghost Hunters deployed, they recorded voices saying, "Cry," and near the Raiders' graves, "I'm still looking for them."

On January 27, 2007, the Henry Ghost Hunters investigated Andersonville. While Kevin explained how most EVPs are taped during ordinary conversations and not when asking specific questions to a spirit, a recorder captured, "Cry." When Andy asked at the Raiders' graves if they had anything to say, an EVP said, "I" or "I'm still." When someone asked if family still visited, a spirit replied, "Yes."

In the archives at Andersonville, Kevin located three old photographs of Providence Springs, taken before modern photo-altering techniques were developed. An exterior shot of men has a number of misty rods entering from both the right and left sides of the frame. Another of the stone springhouse exhibits the same rods and a number of other misty clouds and perhaps a faint human image. The final shot, taken inside the springhouse, shows several rods and what might be a headless angel figure. These decades-old pictures present anomalies commonly captured by today's ghost hunters.

Whatwasthat informed Ghost Hounds that an August 2004 "trip to Andersonville left most of us with a very calm peaceful feeling. Except for the few minutes we thought we were the only four people locked in for the night…We smelled the gunpowder and felt a little creepy around the area of the dead house." She found the town museum and church "very active." Although she had never been there before, she captured an EVP that said, "Welcome back." The team had camped there three years earlier. "Seems these spirits have a great memory," she commented.

Another Ghost Hound, Hauntedandhunted remembered a sixth-grade field trip to Andersonville where he "had eerie feelings, a heaviness, almost a despair that knotted in the pit of my stomach. At one point, I walked through a cold spot that made my hair stand on end." His interest in the paranormal was sparked by incidents like that.

Shadows Among Us

Tom and Margaret Hebert are Michigan natives who moved to Americus. In August 2002, two cousins, Bev Pasden and Molly Reiser, visited. They had heard accounts of haunted Andersonville, so the four traveled to the prison site, where pictures taken in the stockade showed some anomalies. Photographs of the lush, grassy area showed no green, only red clay, the 1864 landscape, and a single horse hoof. "If this is the case," stated their website, "then where is the rest of the horse? This has us puzzled; there was nothing there when the picture was taken."

The Heberts returned in November 2003, and in one picture of Tim, his gray and black sweater appeared blue and white, and his body and legs were distorted, although the remainder of the photo was properly focused.

The Heberts were "able to capture some thick greenish coloring on the ground at the stockade site." Rudy Adams, president of Georgia Paranormal Research Council, believes they "captured a time warp." Another caught "the image of a man's head wearing a hat."

At Andersonville National Cemetery, where the temperature was in the sixties, a reporter with the Heberts pointed a thermometer gauge at several graves. The registered temperature dipped to twenty-six, and through the view screen of digital cameras, members saw "spirit balls" invisible to the naked eye. At an escape tunnel, a photo revealed a ball of light larger than a human head. A closer inspection showed a number of balls concentrated around Tom. Ten feet away Margaret's hands became "like ice" and a photograph revealed several spirit balls on her.

ANDERSONVILLE VILLAGE

In the Andersonville town cemetery, a tape recorder captured sounds of dogs barking "and the sound of a train coming…the closer it got, the louder it sounded" before it "faded similarly." The Heberts said the sounds were of hounds used to track escaped prisoners and a train arriving with additional prisoners, who marched from the town to the stockade.

In a cemetery behind Pennington St. James Church in Andersonville, Tom photographed a grave, only to find his energy level abruptly dropped. He then detected the smell of death and asked Margaret whether she also smelled it. She didn't, but she knew something was wrong and said, "We've got to get out of here." As they left, Margaret's left foot went weak, and Tom suddenly felt a chill. In front of the Andersonville post office, she saw an indistinct person dressed in a floor-length black coat and a black cowboy hat.

The Heberts have published a book, *Shadows Among Us*, which details their paranormal experiences.

Many visitors to Andersonville have physically felt the suffering of the desperate, ill and dying; experienced cold spots at Providence Spring and Stockade Creek; and seen fogs, shadows and even soldiers reaching out to them. Union reenactors often feel welcomed as they enter the site. Whatever paranormal forces originated at Andersonville remain today.

CONCLUSION

The vast area composing Central Georgia and Savannah is sometimes called the "other" Georgia, which is that large segment of the state not included in Metropolitan Atlanta. The region has a number of great cities, innumerable smaller towns and extensive rural areas that thrive economically and culturally and have their own unique histories. Sometimes it seems as though heritage is more alive there, more central to the lives of individuals and families, and the historic sites and landscapes less impacted by modern development and more important to everyday life than in busy metropolises.

The ghosts of central Georgia—west, south, east and coastal—are more historic in nature, more known and accepted and even expected. From an early age, everyone learns what is haunted and who the ghosts might be. They know because their grandparents told them, and the stories were old when granny and papa first heard them from their ancestors. These ghosts are less feared and instead are simply a part of life.

The Civil War impacted this region as much as it did Northern Georgia and Atlanta. The battles might have been fewer and smaller, but Sherman's March burned a vast path across the state, leaving a scar more felt that seen. Not only did local citizens fight and sacrifice during the war, but many were also left hungry and destitute. In this area, the war seems more personal, recent and relevant.

The Civil War ghosts and other paranormal activity of Central Georgia and Savannah are a reminder of a storied history not soon forgotten.

HAUNTED PLACES
OPEN TO THE PUBLIC

Listed in order as they appear in text.

Gaither Plantation
270 Davis Ford Road, Covington, Georgia 30014
(678) 625-1200
www.gaitherplantation.com, thenderson@co.newton-ga.us

Oxford College of Emory University
810 Whatcoat Street, Oxford, Georgia 30054
(770) 784-8888
http://oxford.emory.edu

Georgia's Old State Museum, Georgia Military College
201 East Greene Street, Milledgeville, Georgia 31061
(478) 453-1803
http://www.oldcapitalmuseum.org

Old Governors Mansion
120 South Clark Street, Milledgeville, Georgia 31061
(478) 445-4545
http://www.gcsu.edu/mansion

Magnolia Springs State Park
1053 Magnolia Springs Drive, Millen, Georgia 30442

APPENDIX

(478) 982-1660
http://gastateparks.org/info/magspr
Fort McAllister State Historic Park
3894 Fort McAllister Road, Richmond Hill, Georgia 31324
(912) 727-2339
http://gastateparks.org/info/ftmcallister

Fort Pulaski National Monument
Highway 80 East, P.O. Box 30757, Savannah, Georgia 31401-0757
(912) 786-5787
www.nps.gov/fopu
FOPUAdministration@nps.gov

Old Fort Jackson
1 Fort Jackson Road, Savannah, Georgia 31404
(912) 232-3945
ttp://www.chsgeorgia.org/Old-Fort-Jackson.html
fortjackson@chsgeorgia.org.

Laurel Grove Cemetery
802 West Anderson Street Savannah, Georgia 31401
(912) 651-6772

Hamilton Turner House
330 Abercorn Street, Savannah, Georgia 31401
(912) 233-1833; (888) 448-8849
www.hamilton-turnerinn.com
info@hamilton-turnerinn.com

The Marshall House
123 East Broughton Street, Savannah, Georgia 31401
(912) 644-7896; (800) 589-6304
www.marshallhouse.com
info@marshallhouse.com

Green-Meldrim House, St. John's Church
14 West Macon Street, Savannah, Georgia 31401-4356
(912) 233-3845
http://www.stjohnssav.org/

Moon River Brewing Company
21 West Bay Street, Savannah, Georgia 31401
(912) 447.0943
www.moonriverbrewing.com
info@moonriverbrewing.com.

Juliette Gordon Low Birthplace
10 E Oglethorpe Ave, Savannah, Georgia 31401
(912) 233-4501, Fax: (912) 233-4659
http://www.juliettegordonlowbirthplace.org
info@juliettegordonlowbirthplace.org

Jekyll Island Club Hotel
371 Riverview Drive, Jekyll Island, Georgia 31527
(855) 535-9547, Fax: (912) 635-2818
http://www.jekyllclub.com
mail@jekyllclub.com

1842 House
353 College Street, Macon, Georgia 31201
(478) 741-1842; (800) 336-1842
www.1842inn.com
management@1842inn.com

Hay House
934 Georgia Avenue, Macon, Georgia 31201
(478) 742-8155
www.georgiatrust.org.

Cannonball House
856 Mulberry Street, Macon, Georgia 31201
(478) 745-5982
www.cannonballhouse.org
info@cannonballhouse.org

Ocmulgee National Monument
1207 Emery Highway, Macon, Georgia 31217

(478) 752-8257
www.nps.gov/ocmu.
LaGrange College
601 Broad Street, LaGrange, Georgia 30240
(706) 880-8000
www.lagrange.edu

Bellevue
204 Ben Hill Street, LaGrange, Georgia 30240
(706) 884-1832
http://lagrangechamber.com/clientsites/Bellevue.html
chris@bellevuelagrange.com

Jefferson Davis Memorial Historic Site
338 Jeff Davis Park Road, Fitzgerald, Georgia 31750
(229) 831-2335
GeorgiaStateParks.org/JeffersonDavis.
Because of budget cuts, always call or e-mail for hours.

Andersonville National Historic Site
496 Cemetery Road, Andersonville, Georgia 31711
(229) 924-1086; (229) 924-0343
www.nps.gov/ande

GHOST TOURS

Ghost tours have been a popular form of historical entertainment for many years, and they often incorporate paranormal tales relating to the Civil War. Savannah has been crowned as America's most haunted city and has a number of tours, both walking and motorized. Ghost-tour operators, like ghost-hunting organizations, rise and fall frequently, so check to see what is currently available in your area of interest, particularly around Halloween.

BIBLIOGRAPHY

BOOKS AND MAGAZINES

Alan, Ian. *Georgia Ghosts: They Are Among Us*. Los Angeles, CA: Sweetwater Press, 2005.

Asfar, Dan, and Edrick That. *Ghost Stories of the Civil War*. Alberta, Canada: Ghost House Books, 2003.

Barber, Christian A. Barber. *Spirits of Georgia's Southern Crescent*. Atglen, PA: Schiffer, 2008.

Behrend, Jackie. *Ghosts of America's East Coast*. Birmingham, AL: Crane Hill Press, 2001.

Belanger, Jeff. *Ghosts of War: Restless Spirits of Soldiers, Spies, and Saboteurs*. Franklin Lakes, NJ: New Page Books, 2006.

Brown, Alan. *Ghost Hunters of the South*. Jackson: University Press of Mississippi, 2006.

———. *Haunted Georgia: Ghosts and Strange Phenomena of the Peach State*. Mechanicsburg, PA: Stackpole Books, 2008.

———. *Stories from the Haunted South*. Jackson: University Press of Mississippi, 2004.

Caskey, James. *Haunted Savannah*. Savannah, GA: Bonaventure Books, 2005.

Cobb, Al. *Danny's Bed*. Savannah, GA: Whitaker Street Press, 2002.

———. *Savannah's Ghosts*. Savannah, GA: Whitaker Street Press, 2001.

Coleman, Christopher, K. *Ghosts and Haunts of the Civil War*. Nashville, TN: Rutledge Hill Press, 1999.

Curry, Pat. "Ghost Tales." *Online Athens*, October 29, 1998.

Davidson, Bailey. "Haunted Halls of Augusta State University." *Augusta Magazine* (October 2006).

DeBolt, Margaret. *Savannah Specters and Other Strange Tales*. Virginia Beach, VA: Donning Company, 1993.

Duffey, Barbara. *Angels and Apparitions: True Ghost Stories from the South*. Eatonton, GA: Elysian Publishing Company, 1996.

———. *Banshees, Bugles and Belles: True Georgia Ghost Stories*. Berryville, VA: Rockbridge Publishing Company, 1999.

———. *Miracles from Heaven*. Eatonton, GA: Elysian Publishing Company, 1998.

Farrant, Don. *Ghosts of the Georgia Coast*. Sarasota, FL: Pineapple Press, 2002.

"Guide to Haunted Places of the Civil War." *Blue & Gray Magazine* (1996).

Irby, Mary Lee. *Ghosts of Macon*. Macon, GA: Vestige Publishing, 1998.

Johnson, Scott A. *The Mayor's Guide: The Stately Ghosts of Augusta*. Augusta, GA: Harbor House, 2005.

Jordan, Julie Phillips. "Happy Hauntings." *Online Athens*, October 31, 1999.

Miles, Jim. *Civil War Sites in Georgia*. Nashville, TN: Rutledge Hill Press, 1996.

———. *Fields of Glory*. Nashville, TN: Cumberland House, 2002.

———. *To the Sea*. Nashville, TN: Cumberland House, 2002.

———. *Weird Georgia*. Nashville, TN: Cumberland House, 2000.

Perkerson, Medora Field. *White Columns in Georgia*. New York: Rinehart & Company, 1952.

Roberts, Nancy. *Georgia Ghosts*. Winston-Salem, NC: John F. Blair, 1997.

———. *Ghosts from the Coast*. Chapel Hill: University of North Carolina Press, 2001.

Sallee, Scott E., ed. "Camp Talk." *Blue & Gray Magazine* (October 2000).

Sanders, Michael. *Strange Tales of the Civil War*. Shippensburg, PA: Burd Street Press, 2001.

Schott, Thomas E. *Alexander H. Stephens of Georgia: A Biography*. Baton Rouge: Louisiana State University Press, 1988.

Smith, Gordon Burns, and Anna Habersham Wright Smith. *Ghost Dances and Shadow Pantomimes: Eyewitness Accounts of the Supernatural from Old Georgia*. Vol. 1. Milledgeville, GA: Boyd Publishing, 2004.

Spaeth, Frank, ed. *Phantom Army of the Civil War*. New Jersey: Castle Books, 1997.

Street, Eugenia Wooton. *Yesterday at Tift*. Doraville, GA: Foote & Davies, 1969.

Taylor, Troy. *Spirits of the Civil War*. Alton, IL: Whitechapel Productions Press, 1999.

Thomas, Kathleen. "Haunted Hotel." *Creative Loafing: Savannah,* October 30, 1999.

Toney, B. Keith. *Battlefield Ghosts.* Berryville, VA: Rockbridge Publishing, 1997.

Turnage, Sheila. *Haunted Inns of the Southeast.* Winston-Salem, NC: John F. Blair, 2001.

Visions of Ghost Armies, Real-Life Encounters with War-Torn Spirits (from the Files of FATE *magazine).* New York: Barnes & Noble, 2003.

Walker, Caprice, and Dan Brooks. *Haunted Memories of McDonough, Georgia.* McDonough, GA: McDonough Haunted History Tour and Bell, Book & Candle Used Book Store, n.d.

Walls, Kathleen. *Georgia's Ghostly Getaways.* N.p.: Global Authors Publications, 2003.

Wangler, Chris. *Ghost Stories of Georgia: True Tales of Ghostly Hauntings.* Auburn, WA: Long Pine Publishing International, 2006.

Windham, Kathryn Tucker. *13 Georgia Ghosts and Jeffery.* Tuscaloosa, AL: University of Alabama Press, 1973.

Winer, Richard, and Nancy Osborn Ishmael. *Haunted Houses.* New York: Bantam, 1979.

————. *More Haunted Houses.* New York: Bantam, 1983.

VIDEOS

"Haunted Fort Pulaski." Produced by Steve Kroopnick. *Scariest Places on Earth.*

Haunted Savannah. A&E Television Network, 1996.

ABOUT THE AUTHOR

Jim Miles is author of seven books of the Civil War Explorer Series (*Fields of Glory*, *To the Sea*, *Piercing the Heartland*, *Paths to Victory*, *A River Unvexed*, *Forged in Fire* and *The Storm Tide*), *Civil War Sites in Georgia* and two books titled *Weird Georgia*. The History Book Club has featured five of his books, and he has been historical adviser to two History Channel documentaries. He has a bachelor's degree in history and a Masters of Education degree from Georgia Southwestern State University in Americus. He taught high school American history for thirty-one years. Over a span of forty years, Jim has logged tens of thousands of miles exploring every nook and cranny in Georgia and Civil War sites throughout the country. He lives in Warner Robins, Georgia, with his wife, Earline.

Visit us at
www.historypress.net
....
This title is also available as an e-book